Panama City Beach

Panama City Beach

Tales from the World's Most Beautiful Beaches

Jeannie Weller Cooper

The History PRESS

Published by The History Press
Charleston, SC 29403
www.historypress.net

First published 2011

Manufactured in the United States

ISBN 978.1.60949.141.3

Library of Congress Cataloging-in-Publication Data

Cooper, Jeannie Weller.
Panama City Beach : tales from the world's most beautiful beaches / Jeannie Weller Cooper.
p. cm.
Includes bibliographical references and index.
ISBN 978-1-60949-141-3
1. Panama City Beach (Fla.)--History--Anecdotes. I. Title.
F319.P25C67 2011
972.87'31--dc22
2011005030

Contents

Acknowledgements

I present the work to the public, as best as I have been able to render, and I trust that the leading facts and outlines will be found generally correct. The style and manner has occupied less attention than the subject deserves, but had the author abilities, he has not had the leisure to improve them.
—John Lee Williams, author of 1837 Territory of Florida

All mistakes are the responsibility of this writer and editor, Jeannie Weller Cooper. This is a work using contemporary writings to entertain the reader interested in the east end of Panama City Beach. Contributors were gracious in sharing stories and materials, and it is the hope of the editor that the reader will enjoy contrasting essays on the subjects herein.

The editor would like to offer praise and thanksgiving to the One who has set her in such a spacious place. Great thanks go to the Bay County Library Local History Room. All of the staff and volunteers there have made this book possible in every way imaginable, including providing photographs, reference material, technical assistance, contacts and especially great support and friendship. Thanks especially to Rebecca Saunders for all manner of expertise shared; Anita Lucas for quiet, smiling competence in every situation, and lots of laughs besides; and Cindy Lantis, Adele Head, reference, Bettina Mead, events, volunteers and donors, Jane Becker, Angela Lewis, Ellen Rumph, Jack Cutchens and Lyn Hindsman. Additionally, anyone who has ever donated materials or photographs to the Local History Room Collection has the editor's undying gratitude, as do the aforementioned employees and volunteers and their predecessors, Rose Hughes, Gail Layton and Theresa Hill. This room at the Bay County Public Library is a regional treasure, and the reader will enjoy a visit there immensely.

Thank you for your contributions, the laughs and the encouragement: George Baker, Mrs. Lyn Banks, Susan Bell, Carl Bennett, Ralph and Dorothy Bingham, Jack Bishop, David Brose, Robert Cain, John Daniel, Carl Deen, Ginger Glass Dempsey, Virginia Dixon, Cecil Dykes, Nancy Bryant Burbage Elliott, Larche Hardy, Alvin Hill, Captain Richard Holley, Ann Pratt Houpt, Robert Hurst, Melani Ivey, Frances Jennings, Ken Karr, Marie Bryson Kelly, Frances McConnell, Don McCoy, James Murphee, Johnny Owens, Dennis Pledger, Mrs. Roberta, Toni Shamplain, Francis Sheppard family, Pensacola, Orlando, Claudia Collins Shumaker, Sally Sinclair, John Starling, Adam Watson, Glenda Walters, Mrs. Phil (Betty) Wentzel, Nancy White and Marlene Womack.

Ellen Jennings (Rumph) and cousin Duncan McQuagge palling around Panama City Beach, 1943. *Courtesy Ellen Jennings Rumph.*

Many thanks to the reference staff at the Florida State Archives, library staff and technical reference at Florida State University, Panama City Campus, online reference at Strozier Library, Florida State University main campus. I thank Carla, Karen, Lisa, Paula, Brittany, Greg, Terry and Wayne for all their beach lore. Thanks to research assistant Valerie Emmeline Cooper. Thanks to Hedda Cooper. Especially grateful thanks to The History Press editor Jessica Berzon. She has been the soul of professional kindness and has given me so much help and allowed me to benefit from her expertise. Thanks and appreciation to Hilary McCullough for her insightful reading and suggestions.

Introduction

"His style is eminently dry and difficult to labor through, and must ever confine the History to the shelf as a work of reference and to the closet of the painful student." So said Dr. D.G. Brinton reviewing John Lee Williams's 1837 *Territory of Florida*, the first in-depth English language study of Florida.

The words "Panama City Beach" immediately conjure visions of bright yellow sun, bright white sand and clear turquoise waters capped with surf. The names "East End," "Thomas Drive" or "Grand Lagoon" might not be as instantly recognizable, but longtime visitors and locals know that whatever you call it, this little triangle of land has a lot to offer. An early twentieth-century homesteader attempted to name the area "Fairyland," petitioning the post office for recognition. He wrote to the newspaper explaining that the ride of about five miles across the bay from Panama City would "find the mouth of this inland river, [and one would] realize at once [that] Motor boat owners and sailing enthusiasts will find this safe water a paradise for the pleasure of himself, family and friends."

Follow the sun from east to west, through St. Andrews Bay and the Pass, to Shell Island, or one thousand feet into the Gulf of Mexico at the Panama City Beach Pier, now the wildly popular Pineapple Willy's. When confronted with a map, even visitors will discover they've already been enjoying the paradise for pleasure that is the East End. Here's St. Andrews State Park, a Florida State Park named "America's Best Beach" in 1995 by Dr. Beach (Dr. Stephen P. Leatherman). No one misses Captain Anderson's

Marina and Restaurant at the mouth of North Lagoon. The iconic fishing family moved their livelihood out from downtown Panama City in the early 1950s. In 1967, the Patronis family bought the restaurant, which has been consistently voted "Reader's Choice #1 Seafood Restaurant" in *Southern Living* magazine. Jimmy Patronis currently serves the area as a state representative in the Florida legislature. The wreck of the famed Treasure Ship is still standing; the spring 2010 fire unleashed a flood of treasured

A 1962 ad for Captain Anderson's Pier. It's easy to poke fun at this early ad, which reminds you that the restaurant is "Specializing in Sea Foods," but looking at the lovely modern arched glass wall, the reader will remember that the Andersons managed to be an entrenched Bay County fishing family while simultaneously cutting the path to Bay County's future, transplanting a thriving business from the infrastructure of the Panama City Marina to the edge of the rickety wooden bridge leading to Brown's Beach. *Courtesy Local History Room, Bay County Public Library.*

memories from visitors and locals alike of first dates, proms, first bites of seafood. The Treasure Island Marina is next door, and right down the road is one of Panama City Beach's first forays into the condominium market, Treasure Island Resorts. On Newby's Curve, there's a drop of good old Panama City Beach rowdy fun, featuring pool and beer, right across the street from Panama City Beach Access #1.

Like the state of Florida, the East End features the oldest and the newest, the brightest and the shadiest, all in a few square miles. Native Americans camped here in the years before the Spanish, and then the English, began visiting in the sixteenth and seventeenth centuries. The area has always proved a good hideout for fugitives from the enemy du jour: Native Americans fleeing from alternately the Spanish, English or the crackers, slaves from servitude, Yankees from Confederates, Confederates from Yankees, outlaws, rumrunners, the brokenhearted.

In 1929, the first Hathaway Bridge was completed, connecting Greater Panama City to the gulf beach by automobile. Now anyone could go to the beach, anytime. Even so, like the rest of the state, the lagoon and the beach remained a sleepy curiosity until the bombing of Pearl Harbor mobilized the United States to war. As Redfish Point, Beacon Beach and so many communities were sacrificed to Tyndall Army Airfield, Brown's Beach and the jetties were taken over for military observation of the Gulf waters, which did host enemy marine life, as evidenced by the sinking of the *Emperor Mica*, torpedoed near Port St. Joe by a German U-boat in 1942. Third Army, out of Fort McPherson in Atlanta, oversaw operations at what we now know as the state park, while the U.S. Navy had an amphibious training facility up the bay. The World War II military invasion brought the beach attention, growth and a healthy dose of human biodiversity.

As the area began to prosper, residents took note of the benefits offered by a spot with tree-lined deepwater access to the Gulf, with land enough to build a home. The lagoon was close enough to the bridge to get to work and to the kids' schools—most of which were still located in Panama City into the twenty-first century. (The East End now has its own school, Patronis Elementary.) Little cement block cottages began to sprout up along the south side of the lagoon on the eastern portion. In the 1960s and '70s the land on North Lagoon began to be sold off as lots, and comfortable brick ranch homes sprang up. The beach finally got its own high school in the 2000s, when J.R. Arnold High School opened right off Back Beach Road.

More people, more houses, more boats, more fun. By 2007, some lagoon neighbors began to wonder about the well-being of their hidden treasure

This page and next: "There just isn't anything." So answered one of North Florida's premier historical researchers when I asked advice on images depicting the Grand Lagoon area during Spanish exploration. Nevertheless, we've done a fine job imagineering a destination promising excitement, satisfaction, a little danger and, in this interior, circa 1975, award-winning food. Captain Anderson's Restaurant. *Courtesy Marie Bryson Kelly.*

and got together to see what could be done to protect the unique "inland river." This was the genesis of the Friends of Grand Lagoon.

The East End of what is now called Panama City Beach (the entire area of gulf shore in Bay County, not to be confused with the city, which is located to the west since 1970's incorporation) is a neighborhood of contrasts. Some residents would be content to never venture farther than the Publix on Magnolia Beach Road, and there are visitors making annual pilgrimages to the area from Canada and Europe. The ambit's chronicle includes sadness and joy, as well as the most tawdry good times—Club La Vela! MTV!—and absolutely jaw-dropping encounters with nature, like dolphins diving in the surf and great white egrets perched in the grasses.

Come along—we'll take as many as we can get in the car. Let's take a road trip to Panama City Beach, to the old East End, like folks have been doing for thousands of years. We'll see the gorgeous Gulf beach and a quiet marsh habitat, all a step away from the hottest spots known to man—in the sun or out of the sun!

Note: The reader may note, perhaps with frustration, the absence of regular capitalization of the word "Gulf" and the myriad spellings, pluralizations and punctuations of the name given the bay and the earliest named and recorded settlement, St. Andrews Bay. In the introduction of their 2007 publication, *St. Andrews*, Ann Pratt Houpt, in association with the St. Andrews Waterfront Project, lists: St. Andrews, St. Andrews Bay, St. Andrews City and St. Andrew. The geographic area covered in this book is called East End, the lagoon, Grand Lagoon, the Gulf beach, Fairyland, Gulf Beach, Panama City Beach, the city of Panama City Beach and unincorporated Bay County. The barrier islands separating St. Andrews Bay and the Gulf are ever shifting and have claimed a variety of appellations over the years; presently they are, from west to east, Shell Island and Crooked Island. The people who first visited here—Indians? Native Americans? Chatot? Creek? Guests, tourists, summer visitors, snowbirds, spring breakers, ecotourists? The Navy Research and Development Laboratory addressed the confusion in its sixtieth anniversary publication thusly: "Regardless of the official designation, the R&D Laboratory has always been referred to in the local community as the 'Navy Lab.'" As befits its importance to the residents, it comes first with the most names on the beach—eleven—and we still say "navy base." In chronological order, beginning in 1945: U.S. Navy Mine Countermeasures Station; Countermeasures Station; U.S. Navy Mine Defense Laboratory; Naval Ship, Research and Development Laboratory; Panama City Naval Coastal Systems Laboratory; Naval Coastal Systems Center (NCSC); Coastal Systems Station (CSS); Dahlgren Division; Naval Surface Warfare Center; Naval Station, Panama City; and Naval Surface Warfare Center, Panama City.

The author has chosen to leave the writings contained in this book as found as much as the publisher will allow, in the hope that this helps impart the charm of our east Gulf beach friends, whom, in their writings as in most of their dealings, gently resist standardization.

The Tall Men

Students of human behavior usually discover how very little the basics change over time, in spite of cataclysmic events or technological advance. Most humans enjoy light, warmth, beauty and seafood. All of these are to be had in spades on the coast of Florida and certainly here on the large saltwater bay and its shoreline as it meanders out to the dazzling white and verdigris of the Gulf of Mexico. It should come as no surprise to find that this area has been frequented from the time the seas rolled back. There were certainly folks here when the first known Europeans arrived on the north coast of this body of water; the Spanish sailor Alvar Nuñez Cabeza de Vaca described "tall men" existing in the region. Yet scholarship is only recently attaching any significance to occupation of the area. In the twentieth century, marketers preempted the twenty-first's obsession with branding, with "The Forgotten Coast" being suggested as yet another moniker designed to fix the charms of our beach in the potential visitor's mind. Presumably the Overlooked, Misbegotten, Misplaced and Red-Headed Stepchild were already taken. Even one of the modern-day founders and certainly St. Andrews Bay's biggest single fan, booster and benefactor, George Mortimer West, in his volume *St. Andrews, Florida*, states baldly:

> *There does not appear to be much in evidence as to this section having been inhabited by a very large number of Indians known to white men, since they discovered these shores. There are no burial grounds of importance, and the burials appear to have been scattering and what is termed "intrusive,"*

> *in mounds antedating the arrival of those Indians which were found here by the first white explorers. Now and then, in cutting into mounds, and in excavating on the bluffs, remains of these latter day Indians are found. They do not differ in any way from the skeletons of Indians of today.*

West retired from his position as an executive with a Chicago railroad to St. Andrews Bay and, by 1905, had invested heavily in real estate and development. He somehow fails to point out that much of the scattering and cutting is being done at the time of his writing at the turn of the century by the landowners as they quarry the former inhabitants' discarded oyster shells to sell for use as road beds in the nascent towns clinging to the lovely but harsh edge of the bay. Again, de Vaca had recounted that the natives he met in the early 1500s were at times hungry and sick to the point of starvation, there often being "plenty of mosquitoes but little food," in spite of the bounty of marine life found in the streams, the bays and the Gulf. Whether the locals of de Vaca's era or West's were too weak from malarial illness or unable to obtain or store enough fish for their needs is at question; the soil close to this water is sandy and fine and does not readily give up much fruit. In fact, the grandson of the owner of one of the mound properties said his family moved from this shore to West Bay because the soil was "a *little* better. After all, you can't live on just mullet," he laughed.

Clarence Moore of Philadelphia was one of the first to explore this region's topography and its inhabitants' leavings in the age of modern archaeology and anthropology. He came to the shore in 1891 after pursuing natural studies as far back as 1873, when he is thought to have worked with the Harvard University Peabody Museum on the east coast of the state. Moore was working here between 1900 and 1903 and would revisit the area in 1918, as well as making extensive forays into other Gulf Coast overgrown and undeveloped bays, bayous and river systems. One of his strengths as relates especially to what is now Bay County (aside from the fact that he found us here at all) was his insistence, sometimes exasperating to his contemporaries, on treating the Gulf and the Southeast as one interdependent region. Regarding St. Andrews Bay, he was visionary and entirely correct. His work reinforced the linkages pointing to the migration, often seasonal, of the group de jour from the wooded northern Chattahoochee Valley dividing present-day Alabama and Georgia, through the rich-soiled midlands encompassing the Ocmulgee, Lamar and the Kolomoki Mounds, leading down to the shellfish-, mollusk- and mullet-laden waters of the Apalachicola and St. Andrew Bays.

The "Classics in Southeastern Archaeology" series has been brought out by the University of Alabama Press. It was intended to "bring back into print important, pioneering works on the archaeology of the southeastern United States…contain[ing] new…introductions by…experts that provide historical perspective and bring these source materials up to date…editions for professional and amateur archaeologists alike." This rather dry blurb from the UAB Press website does nothing to inform the reader that this series is effectively the reproduced field notes, including maps, diagrams and photographs, taken by Moore and other documenters of the many eye-popping ceramics, skulls and pristine waterways of turn-of-the-century Florida. Modern archaeologists and anthropologists add explication with new findings for current readers. These are highly recommended. Some are quoted here (including much of the above biographical material on Moore), as well as a follow-up by Florida State University students who, in 1969, revisited one of the native sites recorded by Moore at the turn of the twentieth century.

Following are dates in current use to give a general reference for those interested in the pre-European cultures of the southeastern United States:

From the *New Georgia Encyclopedia*, an online reference work of the Georgia Humanities Council, University of Georgia Press, the university system of Georgia/GALILEO and the Office of the Governor.

WOODLAND	1000 BC	Weeden Island	300 BC–AD 1000
	AD 1000	Swift Creek	20 BC–AD 805
MISSISSIPPIAN	AD 1000–AD 1600		

Regarding artifacts, as found in *The Northwest Florida Expeditions of Clarence Bloomfield Moore*, by Moore, David Brose and Nancy White, "In northwest Florida, Early and Middle Woodland Swift Creek complicated stamped designs co-occur [are found alongside] with Santa Rosa and Weeden Island incised [ceramic artifacts.]" The *New Georgia Encyclopedia* writes in its Georgia timeline, "Swift Creek refers to Woodland culture manufactured specific pottery types [that were] carved into a wooden paddle, [and pressed onto a wet ceramic] to stamp design.

"Weeden Island culture [is] found on Kolomoki mound [artifacts and on the] Gulf coastal plain. [In] middle to late Woodland, 300 BC–1000 AD, [find] incised, punctuated, and red painted pottery."

HOLLEY MOUND

Clarence Bloomfield Moore traveled to St. Andrews Bay and its surrounding tributaries and bayous in the years 1901 to 1904, and again in 1918. These are some of his field notes on one of the sites he explored reproduced in the introduction to *The Northwest Florida Expeditions of Clarence Bloomfield Moore*.

> *Holley Mound, Washington County*
> *This mound, about two miles in a westerly direction from Bear Point, in an old field, the property of Mr. John C. Holley, who lives on the place, is about 100 yards from the water. According to Mr. Holley the mound had sustained no previous digging, with the exception of two small holes dug by members of his family, which yielded nothing except a few bones in fragments.*
>
> *This mound, 2.5 feet high and 50 feet across the base, was totally dug down by us. Seven burials were met with, the first 11 feet in from the NE. margin of the mound, on the base as were all with one exception. The remaining burials continued in at intervals until the center of the mound was reached.*
>
> *Burial No. l.—Part of a pelvis covered by a Fulgur perversum having the mortuary perforation. Presumably other bones of the deposit, not thus protected, had disappeared.*
>
> *Burial No. 2.—Small decaying fragments of a femur and of a tibia, side by side.*
>
> *Burial No. 3.—In a shallow grave below the base of the mound were fragments of a skull and bits of two femurs.*
>
> *Burial No. 4.—A small fragment of decaying bone.*
>
> *Burial No. 5.—Bits of two femurs and of one tibia.*
>
> *Burial No. 6.—The remains of a skull.*
>
> *Burial No. 7.—Decaying fragments of a cranium.*
>
> *We believe that other burials had disappeared from the mound through decay, but think such were from the neighborhood of those we have described,*

as no discolored earth or sign of interment of any sort was found in other portions of the mound. Exactly in the same line with the burials, but beginning at the margin in blackened sand, were many sherds, and fourteen vessels, three or four together at times, some whole, some crushed to pieces.

Bones in this mound were in a far better state of preservation than are those usually found by us.

Sowell Mound

These are more of the field notes taken by Clarence Bloomfield Moore on his trip to St. Andrews Bay at the turn of the twentieth century. His work was originally published under the title *Certain Aboriginal Remains of the NW. Florida Coast*. Again, this text is from the introduction to *The Northwest Florida Expeditions of Clarence Bloomfield Moore*.

Sowell Mound, Washington County
This mound, on property of Mr. Jesse Sowell of a small community on St Andrews Bay [property now owned by the United States government], *is in scrub about 1 mile in a westerly direction from* [another area Moore excavated]. *Previous to our visit a trench 12 feet across had been dug from the northern margin of the mound almost to the center. The height of the mound was 4.5 feet; the basal diameter, 50 feet. A great depression whence the sand for the mound had been taken was at its southern margin. All parts of the mound, not before dug, were carefully gone through by us, beginning at the extreme outer limit.*

On the extreme eastern margin burials were encountered consisting of flexed skeletons, bunched burials, scattered bones and masses of bones, one of these masses having no less than six skulls. These burials extended without intermission until the center of the mound was reached. At first the attempt was made to keep count of the burials, but the difficulty to determine where one ended and another began forced us to limit ourselves to a tally of skulls only, and of these there were one hundred and twenty-one.

All burials but three were confined to the eastern part of the mound between the margin and the center, and were, to a certain extent, superficial, lying between a few inches and 2 feet from the surface. Three burials came from the western part of the mound, one 19 feet from the margin, the other two a few feet farther in. Two of these burials were on the base. One was about 2.5 feet from the surface.

The bones in this mound were in a far better state of preservation than are those usually found by us, and in consequence, a number of crania now belonging to the Academy of Natural Sciences, were saved.

Many of these skulls showed great antero-posterior flattening as by compression from boards, while some gave evidence of early constriction by a board, a concave depression being evident. A selected skull from this mound is shown.

FIG. 67.—Skull showing artificial flattening. Sowell mound. (Two-thirds size.)

This fearsome image is captioned, "Skull showing artificial flattening." Moore explored the turn-of-the-century Gulf coast. He excavated artifacts and shared and recorded his findings with the American Anthropological Society. This is a child's skull found in one of several sites in the immediate area known to have served Native Americans as campsites and burial grounds. *Used by permission, UAB Press, from* The Northwest Florida Expeditions of Clarence Bloomfield Moore, *D. Brose, N. White.*

Captain Bernard Romans, who was familiar with this part of Florida writing in the latter part of the XVIII century, tells us that in his time the Choctaws bound bags of sand to the heads of male children. In this mound, however, all skulls which were in a condition to allow determination showed flattening.

All skeletons but one which lay on the back with the legs drawn up under the thighs, were closely flexed, some lying on the right side, some on the, left.

With certain burials were a small number of oyster shells.

With the skeleton of a child were many small shells (Marginella apicina), perforated for use as beads.

A pendant of igneous rock was found unassociated with human remains and a smoking pipe of steatite lay in sand thrown out by previous diggers.

Beginning with the burials and continuing with them until the end, were great numbers of sherds, parts of vessels and vessels unbroken or crushed but with full complement of parts…Thence on, earthenware and burials continued more or less closely associated, a burial at times being almost in direct contact with two or three vessels.

The Sowell Mound for the Now Generation, in Which the Mound Is Re-excavated to Great Effect

This is a brief report of the excavation of the Sowell Mound, believed to be the mound first reported and described by Clarence B. Moore. The fieldwork described here was done during the summers of 1969 and 1970. The project was under the direction of the late Hale G. Smith and R.C. Dailey. The purpose of this paper is to describe the condition of the mound and the human skeletal remains that it yielded.

The Sowell Mound, a Weeden Island Period Burial Site in Bay County, Florida R.C. Dailey and Dan Morse, M.D. Department Anthropology, Florida State University

Named after a previous property owner, the Sowell Mound is located… on St Andrew Bay…in Bay County, Northwest Florida. The mound is situated approximately 70 m from the edge of the bay on land occupied by the [United States government]. *A large stratified midden adjoins the mound and contains rich cultural deposits at least one meter in depth.*

The mound was well know even in Moore's day and had already been disturbed when he began work there. Indeed, in addition to a trench (3.5 m) wide extending from the northern margin to the center of the mound, he reported a "great depression whence the sand from the mound had been taken" at its southern margin.

From time to time a number of amateur and professional archaeologists have worked at the Sowell site and collected cultural and skeletal material, particularly the former. Among the professionals who worked there are Gordon R. Willey, Charles H. Fairbanks, David S. Phelps, and Hale G. Smith.

In his Archeology of the Florida Gulf Coast, *Willey classified the mound as "definitely Weeden Island, possibly only Weeden Island II" (1949:231) and the midden as "mixed" (1949:401).*

After the U.S. Government acquired the property no further excavations were permitted without a Federal antiquity permit. An exception, however, was the work of W. Lamar Gammon. It was through his efforts that the mound was saved from total destruction when the U.S. Navy began experimental activities in the area. Gammon recovered some 6000 potsherds and larger parts of broken vessels, some of which he was able to restore. He also recovered 12 faceless crania and secured a C-14 date of A.D. 610 + 125 years for this site. In 1968, Gammon arranged for the U.S. [government] *to convey the entire collection to the Florida State University Department of Anthropology.*

During the summer of 1969, students in the Department of Anthropology's summer field school collected bone fragments and pottery from the surface of the mound. They also mapped the site and excavated a number of 3 m squares on the eastern and southern perimeter of the mound area, seven of which were completely excavated. The following summer, work continued on the southern perimeter and several trenches were dug, one through the center of the mound, and the other at right angles to it. This was done in an effort to locate the base of the original mound.

No mound strata were located suggesting, as had been suspected, that Moore had literally replaced the original mound with a new one; although, it is acknowledged that it is very difficult to detect stratigraphic zones in the Pleistocene beach sand with which the mound was formed.

When Moore conducted his investigation of the mound in 1902, he stated that it was 50' (15m) in diameter and 4.5' (1.4m) high. In 1969 when the mound was again mapped, pottery and bone fragments were found to encompass a somewhat circular area more than twice the size of the one Moore excavated in 1902 and though irregular and full of

Spanish, English, Spanish, or the "Six Flags" Period†

In 1513, Spanish explorers finally made it to the shores of some islands on their way to claim an Eastern passage—or so they hoped. Instead, they had run upon the toe of an elephant that would in turn have its day in the sun as the mightiest empire on the globe. In the meantime, they called what they'd found for Queen and God and christened it Floride. Just like most stories about the Flower State, the particulars regarding the naming are confused and contradictory but colorful nonetheless. And really, five hundred years later, who cares whether the Spanish mission settlement was named after the lovely flowers growing on the shore or a festival on the church calendar? The Spanish got here and brought us Spanish Mission–style architecture and a few strands of DNA. Their greatest legacy for the South, especially the south Georgia/north Florida area, was their policy of granting freedom to converted Africans who had been enslaved by the English colonists and the related policies toward the native people of the region. The Spanish "offered" them full rights and privileges when they converted to Roman Catholicism. As the centuries—and Spain had La Floride for two or three centuries—rolled on, this inclusive tradition would ensure that the north Florida folks loyal to Spain would defend the land against the depredations of French settlers, English colonists and the brand-

†. Six Flags over Georgia is the name of an amusement park that opened in 1967 in Atlanta, near the banks of the Chattahoochee River. In its early years it stressed the "historical" motif, with heavy emphasis on Georgia's early years under British, Spanish and French flags, as well as harkening back to the good ole days on de plantation. See Tim Hollis's *Six Flags over Georgia* (Charleston, SC: Arcadia Publishing, 2006).

new creature called an American. Rogue Americans were only too glad to run out the Indians—*they* had land and fields and pelts; the "Indians" were oddly just as reluctant to leave these items. Many of the folks—who were called Creeks and Seminoles by the time of American rule in the early 1800s—either high-tailed it down south or hid in the woods and swamps right where they were. Depending on which hostile group came a-calling, they might identify themselves as Spanish, English, American, African or "Indian." After a while, folks moving in from the north, i.e., Georgia and the Carolinas, lost track. The girls were pretty, the boys were strong; to survive in the new land one needed all the help and companionship one could find.

So aside from the oldest city on the continent, the Floridan owes the Spanish for bequeathing us the most diverse and hardy set of genes in the hemisphere, with the most romantic and adventurous stories to accompany them. And we just like a good story. Included here are some good ones that will give the reader some idea of the mindset of the Bay country resident, distilled through the pen of an old-time for-real Florida cracker. Ira Hutchinson was a retired judge and lover of Panhandle heritage who wrote a column for the *Panama City News Herald* in the 1950s. The *News Herald* was the successor to the venerable *Panama City Pilot*, which had been started in 1907 by none other than George Mortimer West. According to a contemporary reviewer, Hutchinson's family collected the *News Herald* writings and published them in the early 1970s. The writer, John Ware (of the St. Andrew town founding family), reviewed the collection in the 1973 *Florida Historical Quarterly*, giving a short, fond biographical sketch, a little scholarly perspective on the tales told, and that is here as well.

In *St. Andrews, Florida*, West gives an overview of the Bay's history and topography. Introducing these tales is his description of some of the barrier islands in the passage between the bay and the Gulf.

Note: "Floridan" is correct; archaic, but still in use in Jackson County, from whence so many of the beach's pioneers came. A Florida cracker is not just somebody in a pickup with offensive bumper stickers; it more refers to people somewhere near the Florida/Georgia state line who have managed to stick it out through all the wars and rumors of wars since Spanish times. Many of these people kept stock on small or large scale; one theory on the origins of the name "cracker" suggests that these folks used whips, which they cracked at the livestock. Another good story. Here are a few more.

From G.M. West's *St. Andrews, Florida*

Sand Island [is] *a small island, three miles from the shore, and about one mile in length. Except some bunches of tall grass (uniola laitifolia), and some scurvy grass, or as it is called here, sea kale, it is totally barren. During summer it is wholly covered with eggs of sea fowl.*

It is possible that the storm that aided materially in the final destruction of St. Joseph in 1841, or that which destroyed the San Blas light house in 1851, might have swept [Sand] *island out of existence, returning its sand to the barrier that is known as Land's End, as the chart of 1855 shows the barrier once more built up at this point. Williams' description relative to this island being covered with eggs of sea fowl, as well as the reference of DeVaca, in his visit to this shore in 1528, shows the great extent of bird life on these early days. This continued until the white man had permanently settled the country, possibly within the last 75 years, when their destruction began, and it has continued until many on these species that were once common here are now never seen on these shores.*

The name "Hurricane Island" does not appear on any of the chart prior to that issued by the government, designated the "Preliminary Chart of St. Andrew's Bay, Florida," dated 1855. It is quite possible that the storm of 1841, or that which swept the coast ten years later, gave this island the name it bears today. Early writers stated that it was quite heavily wooded, and as late as the year 1900 there were quite a few old pines standing along the sand spit west of Land's End, the "Seven Pines," a prominent landmark there, having been the motif for a poem, so named, by a visiting tourist. The name "Hammock" (Williams' map) would indicate that it was hilly, and possible covered with trees. The sand hills on the "Hurricane Island" of the 1855 chart are laid down as very prominent objects.

Preliminary chart of
St. Andrew's Bay
Florida
From a Trigonometrical Survey
under the direction of A.D. Bache Superintendent of the
Survey of the Coast Guard of the United States
Triangulation by F.H. Gerdes Assistant
Topography by G.D. Wise Assist.

Hydrography by the Party
Under the command of Lieut. O.H. BERRYMAN U.S.N. Assist.
Scale 1/40,000
1855

From West's *St. Andrews, Florida*, we learn that Congress was first induced to place fortifications at the entrance of St. Andrews Bay, possibly in part due to tensions with Mexico. Survey work began in 1849, and this map is dated 1855. Its title is unassuming, and a modern reader has to take a minute to examine and appreciate its myriad features. The "Preliminary Chart of St. Andrew's Bay Florida" not only includes explicit tack by tack sailing instructions through the narrow pass (following), but throughout the topography are given the depths of the waters in the Pass and the bay. The map is two tones only, so a chart is provided so colors of the Gulf floor could be noted by the observant sailor navigating through the narrows. The behavior of the tides is described as well. There was no ship to shore radio, much less a cellphone or a GPS to use to call for guidance or help. This amazing piece of paper served as all of those and had the power to save cargo and lives.

> *Sailing Directions Keep in five fms.* [fathoms] *till Sand Bluff bears N. by W. (N.5 degrees W) steer for it, passing between the breakers (which are readily seen on either side of the entrance) till abreast the N.E. end of the Middle Ground between Main Ship and Swash Channels. Haul to the Nd. & Wd. along the shoal which is easily seen by the color of the waters and the breakers. No pilots are to be had and strangers must be careful in crossing the sand bank, which extends from Davis' Point East beyond the end of Hurricane Id* [Island] *then West to West Pass. In clear weather it is plainly visible. The best place for crossing is on the North side abreast of a high bank, where there are no trees. There is 13 feet at low water on the crossing and 15 and 16 feet immediately after getting over. When over, haul to the W.N. Westward, keeping along the Southside of the Northern port of the bank, till up with Davis' Point when haul to the Nd. gradually keeping clear of the Inner Middle on the Port hand. From Davis' Point to St. Andrew's City, the water is deep, steer for the houses and avoid the shoal of Courtney Point, anchor in three fathoms off St Andrews where a pilot for the upper bays may be had.*

Tides

The rise and fall of the tide is usually small. The time and height of high water are irregular & much influenced by the direction & force of the wind. The average rise & fall from 2 months observation from Fort Pickens, Pensacola entrance, in 1852 was one foot. The rise of the highest tide observed above mean low water was 2.1 ft, the fall of the lowest below 0.9 ft. There is generally but one high & one low water in twenty four hours, except for two or three days after the moon's declination becomes nothing, when there are two small irregular tides in twenty four hours.

The Spanish Shanty Cove Treasure

This column, published June 19, 1952, is set in a spot within sight of most downtown Panama City commerce. Judge Hutchinson's weekly articles were widely read and inspired a love of history and storytelling in a generation of readers.

Another story of hidden treasure at Spanish Shanty Cove was to the effect that a Spanish ship with a treasure chest aboard, being hard pressed by an English vessel, tried to make St. Andrew's Bay, first encountered a northeaster and had to tack to reach the entrance of the bay. Observing another vessel bearing down on her with a favorable breeze, the Spaniard was hard put to elude both vessels and turned westward down the Gulf with a quartering wind aft. Before the occupation of Florida by the English, the Spanish had an outpost at Spanish Shanty Cove, commanding a view of the entrance to the Bay and for miles out to Sea. Spanish Shanty Cove was west of the entrance to the Bay, but east of the present entrance opened across the west peninsula recently. [Pass at the jetties, 1934]

As the Spanish vessel realized its peril, the treasure chest was brought on deck and a stout line was secured to it. The Spanish ran down the beach and when opposite Spanish Shanty Cove, in water about twelve feet in depth, on the "green reef" the captain of the Spanish vessel ordered the chest to be jettisoned from the side of the ship, opposite the English Vessels bearing down on him. The chest of gold quickly sank and the line played out attached to it. Before the English ships overtook and captured the Spaniard, the mate and two companions from the Spanish vessel had leaped overboard near Phillips Inlet and swam ashore, unobserved by the pursuers. At night they made their way along the beach to Spanish Shanty Cove.

Next day, the Gulf being calm, they had no trouble finding the rope attached to the treasure chest. They soon secured a line to it and with the help from the Spanish outpost, dragged the chest ashore and rolled it up to the foot of the sea hills and hid it in the sand. Their labors were lost as it soon began to rain and storm and a terrific hurricane came lasting two days; and the high tides and heavy seas buried the treasure, never to be found again.

FLORIDA HISTORICAL QUARTERLY, JOHN WARE'S REVIEW OF *SOME WHO PASSED THIS WAY*, BY IRA HUTCHINSON

The author graduated from Stetson University in 1905 with the bachelor of laws degree and the same year was admitted to practice before the state and federal courts of Florida. This began a long and distinguished career as a practicing attorney, county judge, United States court commissioner, state attorney, and finally circuit judge. His retirement in 1948 ended his active legal career but allowed him time to pursue his lifelong hobby of history. Few if any residents had a more thorough or intimate knowledge of the history of the central counties of the Florida Panhandle and their early settlers than Judge Hutchinson. Combined with this knowledge was the logical and analytical mind of the lawyer, an enduring memory, and the ready wit of the born storyteller. It was the privilege of this reviewer as a youth to have known the judge. This book is a compilation of articles written after his retirement, the entire series of which ran for more than two years in a Bay County weekly newspaper. Each story is said to have a factual basis, many taken from the author's own experiences, some quoted from reports of others, and still others authenticated from old records or documents and written history. The author briefly describes the origin of the early villages and towns on St. Andrews Bay and certain of the pioneers who settled them. Many of the former are now non-existent. He touches on the life and times of the earliest of these pioneers as recounted by his own father and grandfather, both early settlers in Northwest Florida. He tells of the slaves held by his forebears and their friends and neighbors in the Panhandle. And though the memories of the Civil War were recent and often bitter, Union and Confederate veterans settled areas around St. Andrews Bay where they and their descendants lived in peace and harmony. Among his youthful experiences the judge tells of his travels and employment as an "expert" with gasoline engines, then soon to replace sail as a means of propulsion for smaller types of watercraft. So, too, does he venture afield journalistically in writing of certain of the early events of recorded history. But the author is at his very best and most accurate in his articles treating of the local history of the part of Florida he loved and knew so well. As a collection of newspaper stories this work may be lightly regarded by serious scholars. Yet Judge Hutchinson advised and encouraged numbers of candidates for graduate degrees, at least one of whom is known to have cited him extensively in her master's thesis. The absence of footnotes and an index might likewise disappoint those who would expect these scholarly aids. However that may be, it is a delightful little book, to be enjoyed by scholar and layman alike. When Ira A. Hutchinson departed this life West Florida lost a distinguished jurist, an outstanding individual, and a noted authority on the local history of the area in which he spent most of his life. His family deserves much credit for posthumously publishing his work as a lasting tribute to "one who passed this way."

Another column from Ira Hutchinson, "Eliot's Five Foot Shelf," would have been familiar to most 1950s newspaper readers. Charles Eliot of Harvard University proposed that one could obtain a liberal education by reading a selection of books that could be placed on a five-foot-long shelf. The publisher of *Collier's* magazine challenged him and began offering through the popular magazine a set of the chosen titles, which became known as the "Harvard Classics." The set veritably flew off the five-foot shelves and are now in demand for online resale, and they are readily available in their early editions. Adam Kirsch, writing in *Harvard Magazine* in 2001, credits the attainability to the series's immediate popularity. P.F. Collier, within twenty years of the first 1910 publication, would sell 350,000 sets.

Pirates and Buried Treasures

As in the rest of this collection, the spellings and usages in these excerpts have been left as is to the extent possible in order to allow the speakers' voices to be appreciated. If some of these stories are "sailors' yarns," as Judge Hutchinson asserts, the Massalino/Masssalina family is a real entity, living here in Bay County today, most of their history pretty close to what is related here. There are several variations of the spelling of the family's surname; these are left as they are found.

There are many stories of pirates and buried treasures along the North West Coast, handed down for years by tradition and some of them doubtless have some foundation of facts, but many grew out of some sailors' yarns.

The Bahama Channel through which the Gulf stream flows was the route of the Spanish plate ships, to Spain from Mexico and Central America laden with Spanish gold and silver. Sir Francis Drake was given "pirate license" by England to prey upon and plunder the Spanish shipping. Interesting accounts of Drake's voyages can be found in any library in "Eliot's Five Foot Shelf" under the title of "The Voyages of Sir Francis Drake." Of course all ships were dependent upon the winds for motive power as this was long before Robert Fulton was born. The Spanish "prize" ship, relied many times upon skillful sailing and maneuvering till night fall and sometimes taking refuge in some harbor in the Spanish territory of Florida where, if hard pressed, the treasure could be taken ashore and concealed by burying in a secluded spot. When Pirates were likewise hard pressed they resorted to the same practice of concealing their ill-gotten riches in the earth or by sinking them in shallow water at some spot where they could be recovered at a later date.

When a boy, ten years of age, the writer, was spellbound by stories of Jose Massalino. Jose was a Spanish free Negro, who had lived in Japan before coming to St. Andrew Bay. He had sailed the seven seas, beginning his seamanship as a cabin boy and had heard many stories from Spanish sailors of thrilling adventures on the Florida coast. Jose Massalino came to St. Andrews Bay sometime prior to 1832, for he assisted in the burial of ex-Governor John Clark of Georgia in Old Town, St. Andrew, in October 1832. Jose Massalino lived to be one hundred and eleven years old. [Narcisco, known as] *"Hawk", born July 18, 1840, was his youngest son. One of Jose Massalino's stories was about a pirates treasure buried on the east peninsula between Crooked Island Sound and East Bay which would be somewhere in what is now Tyndall Field. The pirates being hard pressed by a Spanish ship off the Pensacola bar made their escape under cover of darkness into St. Andrew's Bay; and into Smack Bayou, near Redfish Point. Next day seeing several sails in the Gulf near the entrance to the Bay, the pirate captain removed the iron treasure chest and had eight of his Negro sailors (peons) carry it inland on hand-spikes and bury it between three live oaks, which marked a triangular spot. Copper pins were driven in the trees, near the ground, pointing toward the spot where the treasure chest was buried. The peons who carried the treasure to the place of concealment were blindfolded in traveling to and from the place.*

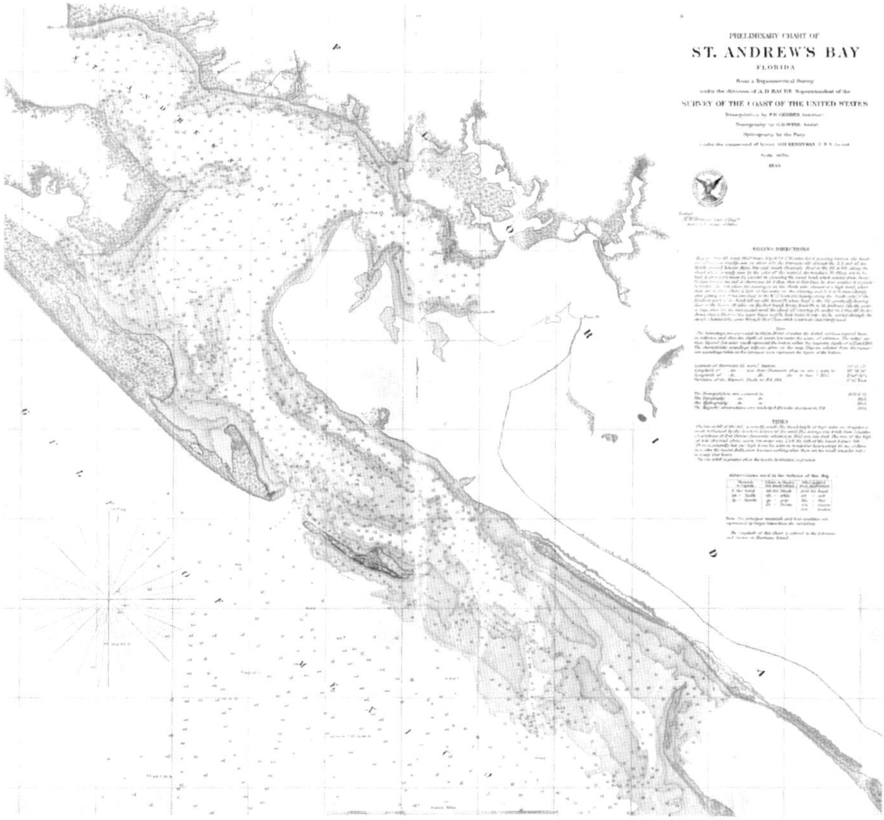

Preliminary Chart of St. Andrew's Bay Florida. This detailed 1855 record of the bay sold for a mere fifteen cents. It included not only a visual representation of the bay but also explicit sailing directions and tidal data. *Courtesy Local History Room, Bay County Public Library*.

At this point in the story Jose would become silent to receive a barrage of questions by his youthful audience. "Did the pirates return? Did anybody ever find the treasure?" To the questions Jose would answer with a questioning shrug of his shoulders and by bringing his elbows close to his side and extending his hands, open palms upward, forward with a quick motion. Then he would answer, "The trees grew and covered the copper pins with new growth and bark." Years and years later, a man came with a crude map and employed Jose to help him hunt the treasure. The map and story had been handed down for several generations of one of the pirate crew but Jose did not think the treasure had ever been found. There were so many trees and so much land to examine.

Always Having to Ask for More Land

Florida has ever a dual nature. It cradles two of the oldest European settlements in the country yet is populated by newcomers. This is not at all a new development; Florida's antebellum years featured the lifestyle of the slow-paced plantation culture of the "Old South" and the lean, rugged guerilla combat of the western frontier, often within miles of each other. One of St. Andrews Bay's first prominent residents epitomizes the conflicts between old and new going on throughout the Southeast. John Clark, always Governor Clark here, was the son of a Revolutionary War hero, Elijah Clarke. He fought beside his father in the 1780s and moved through the ranks, first in the British war and then with militias in fights with the local Creeks living in the "west," i.e., north central Georgia. He was promoted to major general by 1796.

The acrimony between the "Two Georgias" is not a new development, evidently; according to the *New Georgia Encyclopedia*, where much of this biographical information is from, there was much sectional hard feeling between the older, wealthier parts of the state and the newly acquired lands filling with Carolinians. Even though he was an old second-generation Revolutionary War fighter, Clark championed the wooded hill country he was now accustomed to "defending" against the Indians. He participated in political skirmishes with his Lowcountry rivals and was elected to the General Assembly in 1801. When hortatory oratory wasn't enough, he fought a duel with William H. Crawford of the establishment faction and wounded him. Feelings in the old valley parallel to the Savannah River ran high as the cotton; Lucien Lamar Knight in *A Standard History of Georgia and Georgians*—which, by the way, is certainly the template for a history book and a fine read throughout—tells the story in the finest, wryest detail. Crawford, for some reason, steadfastly refused a rematch, so in 1806–7, Clark got at a Crawford associate, Judge Charles Tait, with a buggy whip and "inflicted severe blows upon him with the aid of powerful muscles." Knight continues, "On account of his wooden leg, Judge Tait was no match for his irate antagonist. While the interview was in progress, Tait's horse took fright, but Clark kept along side of him until his wrath was appeased." None of this impeded Clark's career, and in 1819 he was elected to the first of two fairly successful terms as the governor of Georgia.

When he was defeated in 1823 it was by only 623 votes, the *New Georgia Encyclopedia* tells us, and further he retired to a federal post under the wildly popular Andrew Jackson, "Keeper of the Forests," which is how Governor Clark came to be in our story, on our bay. He had a very large home built next to a spring on the edge of the bay across from Courtney Point and Hurricane Island. From his front porch he would have been able to see ships with tall masts full of white sails as they threaded their ways through the inner middle toward the tiny port in the tiny St. Andrews wharf, or north to West Bay. He and his wife, Nancy Williamson, entertained many guests and made neighborly bonds with the Jackson and Washington County planters who brought families during the late summer to rest, frolic and salt mullet for use during the winter and to sell.

There a smattering of folks settled on the water and lived off the bounty of the bay. Some came with knowledge of the sea; some learned. They enjoyed life in a place where one worked and played on the Gulf—with sometimes dire consequences, to be sure—but delightful it was, nonetheless, to make a life on the edge of the water. These are some of the flavors that were put into this gumbo early on: the dependable rhythm of the agricultural calendar, the hot temper and danger of the frontier and the steady, weather-beaten determination of the fisherman.

Governor John Clark died in October 1832 during a yellow fever epidemic most likely brought in on one of the ships made of his "Forest" wood that passed by his front door. His wife died two weeks later. He was buried in a small cemetery near the home with a large marble obelisk of the time period. His home was a Panhandle landmark known for its size, its setting on the sparkling bay and its hospitality. In 1863, Union soldiers came ashore, got into an affray with locals and were avenged by their comrades, who came back to Old Town and burned most of the oldest houses on that stretch of beach, including the Governor Clark house. In 1923, the Daughters of the Revolution came and disinterred his remains, such as they were by that time, and had them established at the Marietta National Cemetery in Marietta, Georgia. From the Marietta National Cemetery website: "Originally known as the 'Marietta and Atlanta National Cemetery,' the Marietta National Cemetery was established in 1866 to provide a suitable resting place for the nearly 10,000 Union dead from Sherman's Atlanta Campaign."

WAR WITHIN A WAR

In this article, first published in the summer 2010 issue of Panhandle glossy *Bay Life*, Jason DeHart recounts lesser-known stories of early nineteenth-century northwest Florida. They don't all make good telling, but these writings do give insight into the events that shaped the attitudes of folks who settled this region. These episodes have led generations of people to either physically hide out in this sparsely populated area or "hide" by denying their background and heritage. Even an armchair genealogist in Bay County will soon run upon stories of folks who only asserted "Indian" lineage in the 1970s, after the "power" movements began to encourage minorities to affirm their group's value.

> *The battles of the Second Seminole war (1835–1842) may have taken place in Central and South Florida, but the region between Pensacola and St. Andrews Bay was ground zero for a little-known but bitter conflict between settlers and Creek Indians. "Walton County was the hardest hit of all the area counties," said Brian Rucker, history professor at Pensacola Junior College. The United States Superior Court failed to hold its regular session in the county because of the disturbances and the economy was seriously disrupted. Rucker's "West Florida's Creek Indian Crisis of 1837," published in a 1991 volume of the Florida Historical Quarterly examines the often unexplored aspects of the Florida War, as the Second Seminole War was known in its day. He described it as a "relatively forgotten chapter in the history of Florida's Indian wars."*
>
> *Andrew Jackson's invasion of Spanish West Florida in 1814 and 1818 dispersed many hostile Creek bands, while others disappeared in the remote woods and bays. When Spain ceded Florida in 1821, settlers encountered these Creeks. Rucker said The 1823 Treaty of Moultrie Creek allowed 800 Creeks to live on reservation lands along the Apalachicola*

River Small bands were scattered from St. Andrews to Choctawhatchee, Blackwater and Escambia bays. Rucker wrote that they hunted, fished, looked for grazing land and occasionally wandered into town for supplies. The white settlers saw the Creek as thieves and rascals who liked to steal cattle. The settlers also believed the Creeks helped and harbored runaway slaves. In the mid 1830s, the settlers felt that Creeks, as well as Seminoles, should be forcefully removed and sent West of the Mississippi. Tensions erupted into violence in 1834, when an 18 year-old white settler was killed in an Indian camp on the Pea River in southern Alabama. A party of white men fought and chased the Indians into the swamps; one Indian was killed and two were wounded.

In December 1835, war began in earnest between the United States and the Seminoles in Florida. In the spring of 1836, as the two sides clashed in the peninsula, troubling news hit the Panhandle: The Creeks were rising near Columbus, Ga. and southern Alabama. Rucker said that panic spread from Columbus to Apalachicola. Florida settlers organized into militias. "White settlers feared that the 'renegade' Creeks, fleeing removal, would travel south to join forces with the Florida Seminoles," he wrote. (Some friendly Creek warriors, however, found their way into the ranks of the U.S. Army. An entire regiment of Creek fighters was enlisted to fight the Seminoles). In East Florida (the land east of the Suwannee River.), efforts by the Army and militia to bring the Florida War to a quick conclusion were frustrated at every turn. Rucker said these setbacks "led to further fears and concerns among West Floridians." In January 1837, more members of the west Florida militia were placed on alert. West Florida became a haven for renegade Creeks driven out of Alabama and Georgia. For decades they had fought amongst themselves but jointly opposed removal efforts, Rucker said. Now the Indians faced economic and social problems that were caused, according to Rucker, by "unscrupulous whites and an unsympathetic federal government." "The fragile 'Creek Nation' fell prey to the old factionalism," Rucker said.

Historian Christopher Kimball said that these problems led to the Second Creek War of 1837. "The Second Creek War in Alabama reached down into Florida as Creek Indians raided plantations and homesteads in the Panhandle area," Kimball said. "In February and March 1837, Creek warriors were defeated at Hobdy's Bridge and along the Pea River in southern Alabama, ending the hostilities of the Second Creek War." Following this defeat, renegade Creeks fled to Florida and formed small bands. Locally, they moved along the Choctawhatchee River into Walton

County, "murdering and pillaging as they traveled," Rucker wrote. Indians attacked and killed members of the Alberson family on Feb. 28, 1837, and one raiding party killed nearly everyone at a homestead in Gadsden County. In response, a mounted militia group from Pensacola searched for Indians along the Yellow River and over to Shoal River. Hampered by impassable swamps and bad weather, they returned empty-handed. However more than 30 Indians later agreed to surrender for deportation west. Relief seemed to be within sight for the people of Pensacola. "It appeared that the majority of the renegades had dissolved into the wilderness north of Choctawhatchee Bay," Rucker said.

But white treachery reared its ugly head in April 1837, when a family of settlers at a Blackwater River lumber mill deceived and captured a family of Creeks, according to Kimball. "Most refugee Creeks were trying to live in peace with the white settlers, and traded for much needed goods whenever possible," Kimball said. "The settlers used this trade against the Indians to set a trap." In the tragic scene that followed, some of the Indians tried to kill themselves rather than be captured.

In reprisal, Creek warriors attacked a group of seven Walton County men along the Shoal River. Only two men survived the attack, and their story whipped Walton County into a panic. "The inhabitants feared for their lives. as well as their crops and livestock."

The local militia pursued the renegades and killed two of them near Shoal River. The back and forth killings made it difficult to convince the Indians to surrender peacefully, but by the end of May 1837, some 70 Creeks had surrendered and were taken west. However, the conflict continued. The same month, Walton County settlers were killed, and territorial Gov Richard Keith Call ordered a militia company from Jackson County to enter the Walton County fray. Citizen soldiers from Franklin and Washington counties were also called up and sent west. The Jackson County militia proved ruthless. In one particularly lethal episode, they wiped out a party of 12 Indians near Alaqua. Those Indians were said to be prisoners, mostly women and children. An Army lieutenant inspected the scene of the massacre and learned that several of the Indians had been scalped, and their earrings cut from their ears. Other militias continued to hound the Indians. On May 19, 1837, Walton County soldiers fought a band of Creeks west of the Choctawhatchee River near what is today the town of Bruce. When the Indians fled into the swamp, the soldiers chased after them. Rucker wrote that the site is still known as "Battle Bay." Three militiamen and about 10 Indians were killed in the skirmish.

A couple of months later, another skirmish took the life of five Creeks and one militiaman.

The constant pressure by the local militias weakened Indian morale. In October, the Indian threat appeared to be over in Northwest Florida, but attacks and counterattacks continued into the 1840s, even after the Florida War was over. The desire by whites to remove the remaining Indians would set the stage for the Third Seminole War in the 1850s. But the Creek uprising of 1837 remains a bitter part of Emerald Coast history. "For the white frontiersmen it was a tragic episode—families brutally murdered, property destroyed and stolen, and settlements terrorized with fear." Rucker wrote about the 1837 violence. "For the Indians it was a more lasting tragedy—many were killed, hundreds were deported to the West, and the remaining natives were condemned to poverty and the loss of their heritage and culture. Atrocities were committed on both sides, and both white and red savages were to be found."

"Hurricane Island"

This feature was written by Marlene Womack and was included in her popular 1998 history of the region, *The Bay Country*. There she notes the earlier usage of the eponymous term for the area leading to and surrounding St. Andrew, North, West and East Bays. I have used the phrase throughout this volume, as it is appropriate and indicative, and I am, as usual, in her debt.

"Hurricane Island" brings to mind thoughts of storm-tossed seas and wind-swept beaches. An island by this name once existed in Bay County at the entrance to St. Andrew Bay in the Old Pass. For 80 years it played an important role in history, then disappeared into the sea.
—Marlene Womack

Until the mid-1800s, Sand Island, Hummock Island and Crooked Island were located at the entrance to the bay. John Lee Williams, a Pensacola attorney, wrote about this area in 1823 and 1827. Williams was one of two men chosen to select Florida's capital site. Williams described Sand Island as being separated from the peninsula that is now Shell Island by a shoal and an eight-foot deep, narrow channel. Except for some bunches of tall grass and scurvy grass or sea kale, as it was called, Sand Island stood totally barren. During the summer, eggs of sea fowl covered the small

Marlene Womack at BooksAlive! Local, 2010. Marlene Womack came to Panama City Beach in 1973, when her late husband was transferred to Tyndall Air Force Base. Her sons enjoyed playing in the surf, and she enjoyed reading back issues of the local newspaper and cataloging local cemeteries. By 1982, her interest in area history led to the long-running and influential column "Out of the Past," published in the *Panama City News Herald*. Womack is the author of six books on the history of northwest Florida, including 2008's *Moonshine Mayhem*, chronicling the area's memories of the quasi-legal liquor trade. *Author's collection.*

island. Hummock Island came next. This island was located 1¼-miles southeast of Sand Island and measured six miles in length. This narrow island contained no timber, but it was covered by tall grass. A ridge of sandhills extended along the west side of the island. Vessels could safely anchor on the north side after sailing through the pass off the eastern end of the island. Crooked Island appeared as the largest island on Williams' map. He listed it as being as long as Hummock Island, but in the shape of a crescent. This island was covered by a big grove of pine trees. Then a severe hurricane struck this section in 1851, changing the coastline. After the rough seas subsided only one small two-mile long island remained at the entrance to the bay. People living here at that time began calling this small piece of land Hurricane Island.

A.D. Bache and E.H. Gerdes surveyed St. Andrew Bay in 1855. During their stay here, the men established an astronomical station on the eastern end of the island at 30 degrees, 4 feet, 23 inches. [The map created is included here, with their detailed navigation guide.] *During the Civil War, Hurricane Island served as utmost importance to the* [Union army] *Eastern Gulf Blockading Squadron, charged with capturing* [Confederate] *blockade runners and destroying saltworks around the bay. The squadron established its headquarters on Hurricane Island, erecting several barracks, a long wharf on the north side of the island where the ships anchored, and a small prison camp. The Saddle Hills, gigantic sand dunes, served as landmarks for ships at sea on what is now Shell Island.*

The first two years of the war Union forces were busy enforcing the blockade and seizing blockade runners such as the steamer Florida and, the sloop Lafayette farther up the bay. But in late 1862, the Yankees turned their attention to demolishing salt works, a commodity needed desperately by the Confederacy after the blockade was imposed. Hundreds of saltworks existed around the bay and its secluded creeks and bayous. Captured saltmakers were given the choice of swearing allegiance to the U.S. Government or of being taken prisoner and escorted to Hurricane Island. Most chose allegiance to the Federal government, but were back making salt within a few days.

On March 20, 1863, the Yankee and Confederate troops fought their biggest local battle. The attack took place at Old Town (near Frankford Avenue and West Beach Drive). Yankees who died were taken back to Hurricane Island for burial in the small cemetery begun a year earlier for victims of yellow fever and seamen dying aboard ships.

On the western end of the island stood the "Government Camps," the stopping place of the many refugees who had came to the Gulf shore to seek protection of the blockading fleet. From these camps many recruits were secured, for the fleet and some of the federal Florida regiments. A small prison camp was also established in the vicinity of Redfish Point.

After the war, some refugees continued to live on the island. In 1878, Hurricane Island was relinquished by the government, but it was set aside again as a military reservation on May 3, 1897.

Shipping increased on St. Andrew Bay with the erection of sawmills and turpentine stills in the early 1900s. During those years a pilot station was constructed on Hurricane Island to house the men who guided the sailing ships in and out of the bay. The five-room pilot house was located on the Gulf side of the island. Pilots such as Thomas Croft, B. Alexander, Jimmy Fuller, W.E. Spiva, Graydon York and Bert Ware had no way of knowing when a vessel was due in port. So each morning the man on duty climbed to the top of the tower to scan the horizon. If he saw the billowing white sails of a ship he took the pilot boat and met the vessel in the sea lanes. Once he had his boat in position next to the ship, he climbed up the long rope ladder and gave the ship's captain the "local knowledge" for sailing the ship into port. By that time, Hurricane Island had decreased in size and measured about one mile long and between one-fourth to one-half mile wide. Because of the rapid rate of erosion on the west and south sides of the island by the wind and waves, the pilots were forced to move their station to the bay side of the island in February 1917. Excursionists from Panama City, St. Andrews and Lynn Haven enjoyed visiting the island during this period. Besides talking and sometimes eating dinner with the pilots, they liked to gather shells, pick sea grass and saunter around the isolated island. But in September 1926, a devastating hurricane struck this section, leveling most of the island and sweeping away the old pilot house. On a trip here after the storm, a visitor penned this poem, entitled "Hurricane Island."

A wind swept isle lies leagues always along
its lonely shore
Of shifting sand and curving bay, the Gulf sends
echoing roar
There, only seabirds make their home, and shrilling
cries hark through the foam.
But when the night winds lie at rest, upon the
Gulfs dark shining breast
A ship sways silently, a breeze at dawn. Some
ripples
Break the long, long reach. The ship glides out
and tiny waves
Break noiselessly upon the beach.

In 1934, the waters of the Gulf finally washed away all signs of Hurricane Island. Today, Hurricane Island remains on Bay County maps. It is shown as the eastern end of Shell Island. But those who remember say the island is actually out in the Gulf off Shell Island. Legend has it that around the turn of the century, an effort was made to move the Hurricane Island burial ground to Pensacola National Cemetery because of the erosion of Gulf waters and the danger of these graves being washed away into the sea. No records can be found to substantiate this move, however. The remains of those who died here during the Civil War most likely lie covered with conch and scallop shells in their watery grave.

A Very Impudent Declaration

The Civil War, the War Between the States—what have you. The state of Florida doesn't immediately come to mind. But Florida had joined the Union in 1845 and was a part of the CSA, if in a uniquely Floridan way. It was the least populated state in the Confederacy, with most of its citizens concentrated in the northeastern corner around St. Augustine and Jacksonville and some spread through the oldest counties bordering Georgia and old Pensacola at the far western tip of the Panhandle.

The wartime governor, John Milton, was actually a Georgian, from an old family there. He was an ardent states' rights supporter and had gained no small advance in Georgia politics, still a stout heart's game and still rent by the same fierce party feeling as in the days of Governor Clark. Milton had been involved in the "pens dipped with vitriol" debating of the day with another politician while living in Columbus, and the argument swung low, with Major Joseph Camp accusing Milton, long married to Susan Cobb, of dalliance with young women. The Code Duello had been criminalized in 1809, not long after Governor Clark's adventures. The spirit was quite nigh, however; one's honor was still very much a part of the social and political scene. For whatever reason, John Milton took a shotgun and shot Camp in the back as he walked down the street and then once more as he lay felled from the first. In spite of the presence of onlookers, Milton was acquitted of murder—for Camp died from the assault—on grounds of self-defense. Being backed by a good group of his fellow partisans saved him in the courts; however, Milton had certainly blown away any hope of a future in politics in

Georgia. Whether to let this infamy die down or for the sheer sake of a new vista, Milton and his wife moved to Mobile and then New Orleans, where their infant daughter and then Susan died; the surviving daughter joined them in death soon after.

John Milton did exactly what many men did in that day under strained circumstances: he went to Texas. He visited with relatives, served in a militia there and married again. He was able to connect with cousins on his mother's side, the Robinson family, and moved to Marianna, Florida, an established farming center. Milton practiced law, acquired land and slaves and settled. He and Caroline Howze would have ten children together. He was not the first Georgian, nor would he be the last, to hie down to Florida and remake himself in the warm sun. In Jackson County, he found a measure of success and renewed his place in society, as he was soon placed as a candidate for state representative. He was on his way to the governorship, which he won in 1861 right in time for the events of April, when the fire-breathing South Carolinians shelled the U.S.-held fort out in the harbor and started the whole bloody mess, which seems to get re-fought with the slightest or no provocation at all.

Even noncombatants thrall at the stories of brother against brother, state against state. Many families have worked through the years to make sure their fathers, brothers, grandfathers and great-grandfathers are not forgotten. Florida furnished salt, since it did not have a huge population to assemble into troops. Its miles and miles of shoreline offered haven for blockade runners attempting to get cotton out of the South to sell for valuable gold and U.S. dollars to buy weapons and supplies. They also brought in supplies and products not available in the South due to the Federal blockade of the Confederacy's coasts.

The State of Florida, not unmindful of the dollar of the history tourist, has continued to oblige petitioners with official roadside signs under the aegis of the Florida Historical Marker Program Division of Historical Resources. These can be seen online at MyFlorida.com, but of course it's more fun to see them in person. There are several markers commemorating the efforts of the people who dried the salt out of the seawater. Salt was used for preservation of food, specifically meat, in an era of very limited cooling or refrigeration. One Bay County sign was placed west of the beach and the bay, on U.S. 98 past Phillips Inlet Bridge. One is directly opposite Dellwood and Magnolia Beaches, looking north across the bay. It's at the intersection of West Beach Drive (U.S. Business 98) and East Caroline Boulevard. It reads:

> *Between 1861 and 1865, the St. Andrew Bay Saltworks, one of the largest producers of salt in the South, contributed to the Confederate cause by providing salt, fish and cattle for southern troops and citizens. A necessary preservative in those times, salt sold for as much as $50 per bushel, and was produced in wood-fired saltworks on the perimeter of the West Bay, East Bay and North Bay and Lake Powell (a.k.a. Lake Ocala). An estimated 2,500 men, primarily from Florida, Georgia and Alabama, were exempted from combat duty in order to labor in the saltworks. The salt was transported to Eufaula, Alabama, then to Montgomery, for distribution throughout the Confederate states. Because of the importance of St. Andrew Bay Saltworks to the Confederacy, acting Master W.R. Browne, commander of the U.S. Restless, was instructed to commence a series of assaults beginning in August 1862. In December 1863, additional Union attacks occurred, which Confederate home guards could not resist. The attacks resulted in the destruction of more than 290 saltworks, valued by Master Browne at more than $3,000,000. The St. Andrew Bay Saltworks employees promptly rebuilt them, and they remained in operation through February 1865.*
>
> *Sponsored by* THE SONS OF CONFEDERATE VETERANS, CAMP 1319 AND THE FLORIDA DEPARTMENT OF STATE

However, by 1862, Governor Milton was truly distressed. In all of his striped background, his belief in the efficacy of the Confederate States working in unison, his loyalty to the cause of states' rights does not seem to have been questioned. William Watson Davis, in his 1913 *The Civil War and Reconstruction in Florida*, reports that something moved Milton:

> *Citizens of Florida and citizens of neighboring states established themselves with kettles on the sea-coast because salt-makers were exempted* [from being drafted into the Confederate army]. *Governor Milton stated "Many able bodied men from adjoining and this state have repaired to the Florida sea-coast, and under the pretense of making salt, have been holding intercourse with the enemy; others have been lazy loungers. I know ten men associated in salt-making on the coast for the past six weeks. They have not made a bushel."*

Governor Milton was not the only distressed party. The Federals made periodic forays onto the north side of the bay, as well as up the North Bay and the creeks, to check salt-making activities. Headquartered on Hurricane

Island, they were quite willing to grab Southern blockade-running boats out of the bay. One early spring day, tensions flared as a group of Union sailors crossed a group of Confederate soldiers. The Florida Department of State and the Sons of Confederate Veterans had this marker placed on the same stretch of West Beach Drive as one of the salt-making memorials to commemorate what has become known as the St. Andrews Bay Skirmish, described below:

> *Near this site on March 20, 1863, Confederate soldiers commanded by Captain Walter J. Robinson repelled a landing by Union sailors led by Acting Master James Folger of the blockading vessel U.S.S.* Roebuck. *The 11-man scouting party of Union sailors was seeking to locate a southern civilian vessel near the "Old Town" spring, when they were reportedly ordered to surrender by Captain Robinson. During the ensuing skirmish, several Union sailors were killed and wounded as they fled to their launch boat. Quarter, or safe passage, was requested by the remaining Union sailors to retrieve their dead and wounded. Total Union casualties were six dead and three wounded. Union sailors buried four of the deceased on nearby Hurricane Island, and a fifth sailor was interred by the Confederate soldiers. No casualties were recorded by the Confederate unit, which later became Company A of the 11th Florida Infantry Regiment. After the conclusion of the Civil War, the remains of the Union sailors were removed to the national cemetery at Fort Barrancas.*

More information, and particularly photos submitted by what are termed "marker collectors," are online at the Historical Marker Database. Interested parties visit and photograph the sign and its surroundings and submit the photo and perhaps a description to the HMDB. The publisher, J.J. Prats, extends a warm "welcome to the excitement of historical marker collecting. Please join me, my fellow editors…in building the most comprehensive catalog of local history on the Internet." A correspondent, Craig Swain of Leesburg, Virginia, submitted a page, including good color photographs, that you may see online, or visit the sign yourself to see the marker. From Craig Swain's HMDB page, an article from the *New York Times*, 1864:

> *OPERATIONS ON THE FLORIDA COAST.; Salt Works near St. Andrew's Sound Destroyed.*
> *Published: May 1, 1864 In the* New York Times, *dateline: Washington, D.C., Saturday, April 30.*

> *The Navy Department has received a communication from Rear-Admiral* B*AILEY*, *commanding the East Gulf Blockading Squadron, giving the details of two expeditions in the vicinity of St. Andrew's Sound, Fla., under the direction of Acting Volunteer Lieut. W.M.R.* B*ROWNE*. *The first consisted of eight refugees, in a dug-out canoe, who ascended Wetappoo River some twenty miles, to White Bluffs, and there destroyed 2,000 bushels of salt, brought away some sacks, and captured a barge 36 feet long, 11 feet beam and 3 feet deep, which he is fitting up with howitzers for further operations. Twenty-three refugees were brought off.*
>
> *The other expedition consisted of two men in boats of the Restless, who proceeded up East Bay. They succeeded in destroying two Government salt works, with 300 bushels of salt.*
>
> *There are five companies of rebel cavalry in that vicinity to guard these works, who rebuild them as fast as they are destroyed.*

In Marianna, Governor Milton was again at the mercy of his strong passions. He is said to have declared, "Death would be preferable to reunion." Governor John Milton died of a gunshot wound, believed by most to be self-inflicted, to his head at his Jackson County home, Sylvania, on April 1, 1865. He was again not the first and would not be the last to discover that even the Florida state line can't hold back some torments.

Stand By the Union

We wrap up our tales of the Civil War in St. Andrews Bay with a fictional offering from William Taylor Adams (1822–1897). He edited Sunday school literature and magazines for children, meaning the better off middle classes that could afford to buy such. These were the LeapFrogs and iPads of their day. Adams wrote serially under the name Oliver Optic for children, as well as other novels for general publication. *Stand by the Union* was published in 1891, and this editor begs the readers' utmost patience. If one will pick through the archaic writing style and tone,* he or she will be treated to a rollicking good time. *Stand by the Union* was part of the series "The Blue and the Gray—Afloat" offered in "Two colors cloth Emblematic Dies Illustrated. Price per volume $1.50." The reader will note this selection features the generous use of the ellipsis points. The fashion of writing in the nineteenth century seemed to approve of the idea that the writer should not settle for three words to recount a narrative when one hundred would suffice.

Whether this mode was influenced by the practice of magazine editors paying writers by the word, this writer does not know. Included here also is Adams's preface, which may help introduce the subject and plot line of the story. As outmoded as the voice may be, a recent scholar has used *Stand by the Union* as a resource in her own exploration of the ages of soldiers serving in the armies waging the American Civil War. Adams writes:

> *Incidents of the story are located in the midst of the war of the Rebellion, now* [1891] *dating back nearly thirty years, or before any of my younger readers were born…Though it is said that the South "robbed the cradle and the grave" to recruit the armies of the Confederacy, it is as true that young and old in the North went forth in their zeal to "Stand by the Union."* [He goes on to assure us of that.] *The boys of to-day read with interest the narratives of the boys of thirty years ago, and listen with their blood deeply stirred to the recital of the veteran…who brought back to his home only one arm or one leg.*

Adams continues, "In the official record of a certain regiment recruited up to the full standard, we find that 47.5 per cent of the non-commissioned officers and privates were under twenty-one years of age. We find a few in the list who were only sixteen and seventeen years…Even boys of fourteen and fifteen were enlisted as musicians, 'drummer boys,' and served out their full term."

So we join our hero, Christy (at that time a common male diminutive for Christopher), an eighteen-year-old set to sail as a newly commissioned officer on the *Bronx*. For the Union. Get it? North. After a series of exciting adventures laced with wry and manly humor, they've made it all the way from New York to the Gulf of Mexico, where Christy has succeeded in capturing a privateer and his vessel, the *Magnolia* (from, of course, the South), at St. Andrews Bay. There is much skullduggery throughout the story involving look-a-like relations on opposing teams, rather Shakespearian, and succeeding generations of sea-goers with the same name, rather like a Russian novel. Relax. Read. Enjoy. The polished but sinister Southern blockade runner, Captain Flanger, whose *Magnolia* has just been captured by Christy Passford, is keeping his first mate in bondage as a slave. The sailor is introduced here:

> *AN EXPEDITION TO ST. ANDREW'S BAY*
>
> *"What is your name, my man?" asked Christy, as he looked over the stalwart form of the skipper of the Magnolia.*

"Michael Bornhoff," replied the prisoner.

*"Are you a Russian?" asked the commander, inclined to laugh at this singular name of one of the proscribed race.**

"No, sir; but I was named after a Russian sailor Captain Flanger picked up in Havana. I don't mean this Captain Flanger that was on board of the Magnolia, but his father," replied the stout fellow.

"Are you a free man?"

"No, sir; I belong to Captain Flanger: his father is dead, and left me to his son."

"Why did you bless the Lord that you were here at last?"

"Because I have been trying to get here for more than a year," replied the contraband, after looking about him for a moment, and then dropping his voice as though he feared Captain Flanger might hear what he said. "Now, mister, will you tell me who you are before I say anything more? for I shall get my back scored with forty-nine stripes if I open my mouth too wide;" and again he looked timidly around the deck.

"You are on board of the United States steamer Bronx, and I am the commander of her," replied Christy, desiring to encourage Michael Bornhoff to tell all he knew about the expedition in the Magnolia.

The skipper took his cap off, and bowed very low to Christy when he realized that he was talking to the principal personage on board of the gunboat. He was well dressed for one in his position, and displayed no little dignity and self possession. Perhaps, if he had not been tainted with a few drops of black blood in his veins, he might have been a person of some consequence in the Confederate service.

"Not a bad wound at all, Captain Passford," said Mr. Pennant. "The doctor says I am still fit for duty."

"Captain Passford!" exclaimed Michael Bornhoff, as he heard the name; and the third lieutenant passed on to take a look at the prisoners.

"That is my name," added Christy, smiling at the earnestness of the skipper.

"That is a bad name for this child," said the octoroon, shaking his head. "Are you the son of Colonel Passford?" [Christy's uncle, who lives in the—da-dum—South.]

"I am not; but I am his nephew," replied the commander, willing to be perfectly frank with him.

"Bless the Lord that you are his nephew and not his son!" exclaimed Michael fervently, as he raised his eyes towards the sky, which was beginning to be visible through the fog. "I have heard about you, for I was

to pilot a vessel out of Cedar Keys when you came up there in command of the boats. Colonel Passford was over there, and he saw you on board of the Havana."

"Then we understand each other, Mr. Bornhoff," added Christy.

"Perfectly, Captain Passford; and I would trust you with my freedom, which is the dearest thing on earth to me. But don't call me 'mister,' or you will make me forget that I am a n-," said the skipper, laughing in his delight* [evidently persons with "black blood" laugh quite often, under any and all circumstances, according to this reading] *to find that he was in good and safe hands. "Captain Flanger called me Mike always, and that is a good enough name for me."*

"Very well, Mike; you are a free man on board of this ship."

"I ought to be, for I am a whiter man than Captain Flanger." [Good one, Mike!]

"Now tell me what you know about that expedition on board of the Magnolia," said Christy more earnestly. "Mr. Pennant reports that your passengers claimed that they were peaceable citizens, and that your sloop was bound to Apalachicola. Was that true?"

"Just then they were peaceable enough; but they were not when Captain Flanger ordered them to fire on your men. Colonel Passford and I were the only peaceable citizens on board of the sloop, and I was no citizen at all," replied the skipper, laughing.

"You are one now, at any rate. Were you bound to Apalachicola?"

"Not just then, captain," chuckled Mike, who seemed to be amused and delighted to feel that he was telling the secrets of his late companions. "We were going to Apalachicola after a while, where we were to pilot out some vessels loaded with cotton."

"Then there are cotton vessels at that port, are there?" asked Christy, pricking up his ears at this suggestion.

"Half a dozen of them, and a steamer to tow them to sea."

"Are you sure of this information, Mike?"

"I did not see them there, Captain Passford; but it was your uncle's business to look after them, as he was doing in St. Andrew's Bay." [Translation: Hey, don't ask me if you already know the answer.]

"Then my uncle has vessels in that bay which are to run out?" inquired Christy, deeply interested in the revelations of the skipper.

"Only one, sir: a steamer of five hundred tons, called the Floridian."

"Precisely; that is the vessel we are after. But what was my uncle doing on board of your sloop, with Captain Flanger and the rest of your party?"

"My master was the captain of the Floridian, and we came out here to see if there was any blockader near, that had come up in the fog. The steamer was to be brought out by the pilot, who has been on board of her for three days."

"Who were the men with muskets on board of the sloop?"

"Those were the coast guard, sir," replied Mike, chuckling again.

"The coast guard? I don't understand that," replied Christy, puzzled at the expression. [Must be some "navy humor." Sneer. "The Coast Guard? Who are they?"‡]

"Eight of them, sir; and they have been keeping guard on Crooked, St. Andrew's, and Hurricane Islands, to let them know inside if there was any blockader coming this way. They had skyrockets and flags to make signals with."

"But why were they brought off if the steamer is still in the bay?"

"The Floridian was coming out this morning in the fog, if Captain Flanger made the signal for her to do so. Then the captain was to go on board of her, and I was to sail the rest of the party to Apalachicola," replied Mike, still chuckling with delight at his ability to give the commander such important information.

"Then the Floridian is all ready to come out of the bay?" asked Christy, suppressing the excitement he was beginning to feel.

"All ready, sir; and the signal was a skyrocket, which the pilot could see over the fog."

"We will not give them any signal, but we will treat them to some visitors. Is the steamer armed, Mike?"

"No, sir; not a single big gun, and she has only hands enough to work her. Steam all up when we came out of the bay, sir," said Mike, laughing heartily, apparently in spite of himself.

"Call all hands, Mr. Camden," said the commander in brusque tones...

"Mr. Flint," called the commander to the first lieutenant, as soon as the crew were assembled on deck, "there is a steamer of five hundred tons in St. Andrew's Bay, all ready to come out at a given signal from the party just captured by the first cutter. I propose to capture her with the boats, and you

‡. Actually, Captain Christopher Passford's confusion is understandable. According to its official website, "The United States Coast Guard...trace[s] our history back to 4 August 1790, when the first Congress authorized...vessels to enforce tariff and trade laws and to prevent smuggling. Known variously through the nineteenth and early twentieth centuries as the Revenue Marine and the Revenue Cutter Service." It only received the name "Coast Guard" in 1915 after merging with the Life Saving Service. The website's "History" leaves the reader with this little thrust: "The Coast Guard is one of the oldest organizations of the federal government and, until the Navy Department was established in 1798, we served as the nation's only armed force afloat." So, there.

will take the command of the expedition. The first and second cutters will be employed, and you will see that they are ready." [Etc., etc…]

"What am I to do, Captain Passford?" asked Mike, who was watching the proceedings on deck with the most intense interest. "I want to ship in the Yankee navy as a pilot, for I know this coast from the Mississippi to Key West."

"Are you a sailor?" asked Christy.

"I went to sea for eleven years, and Captain Flanger, father and son, put my wages in their pockets."

"You cannot ship as a pilot, only as an able seaman, if you know how to hand, reef, and steer, and how to make knots and splices."

"I know all that, captain, like I know my name."

"Then I will look upon you as an able seaman until you are formally enlisted. Mr. Flint, this man is Michael Bornhoff; he is an able seaman and a pilot in these waters. I think you had better take him with you, for he is fully informed in regard to the Floridian, which you are to bring out. Let him have pistols and a cutlass," said Christy.

[Christy, the] *commander walked back and forth, considering the information he had obtained from the skipper of the Magnolia, of the correctness of which he had no doubt, for Mike impressed him as a truthful man, and, like all the contrabands, his interest was all on the side of the Union, which meant freedom to them. For the first time he* [Christy] *began to feel not quite at home in his new position. He had been compelled to fight for it; but he absolutely wished that he were the first or second lieutenant rather than the commander of the vessel.*

[more etc., etc…]

He had learned that several vessels were loading with cotton at Apalachicola, with the intention of running the blockade, if there was any blockader off Cape St. George. His uncle Homer [Colonel Passford] *was engaged in superintending the fitting out of these vessels, though whether on his own account or that of the Confederacy, he was not aware. Christy felt that he ought to follow up the information he had obtained with decided action; but he was hardly in condition to do so, for he had fifteen prisoners on board, and he would be obliged to send a prize crew off in the Floridian when she was brought out, as he was confident she would be. He could not settle the question at once, and he went down into his cabin, where his uncle was waiting very impatiently to see him, and had asked Dave a dozen times in regard to him.*

Colonel [Uncle Homer] *Passford was naturally very anxious to ascertain what had been done, and what was to be done, by the Bronx; but the steward was too discreet to answer any of his questions, and* [Colonel Homer Passford] *was not aware that his son Corny* [Passford, Christy's look-a-like] *was a prisoner on board as well as himself.*

Chapter XXI

A Non-Combatant on Board the Bronx

Colonel Passford was reclining on the divan when the commander entered the cabin; but he rose to his feet as soon as he saw his nephew. Christy thought he looked thinner and paler than when he had last seen him. He was now only forty-two years old, but he looked like a man of fifty.

"I have been wanting to see you, Christy," said the planter, as he approached his nephew. "I learn, with no little astonishment, that you are the commander of this steamer."

"I am, uncle Homer," replied the young man.

"Then you can tell me better than any one else in regard to my status on board of the Bronx," added the colonel, who had won this title years before in the militia. "Am I considered a prisoner of war?"

"I do not so consider you, uncle Homer; but I cannot say how my superior officer will look at the matter when I report to him. You were taken in a sloop that fired upon the first cutter of the Bronx, wounding one of the crew and the officer in command."

"That was the folly of Captain Flanger; and I protested the moment I discovered what had been done," added the planter, who seemed to be anxious to relieve himself of all responsibility for the discharge of the muskets.

"Were you in charge of the sloop, uncle Homer?"

"I was not; I had nothing to do with the sloop. She belonged to Captain Flanger."

"Who is Captain Flanger?" asked Christy.

"You have him on board, and perhaps he had better answer the question himself," replied Colonel Passford with a smile.

"It was a superfluous question, for I know all about him. He is the captain of the Floridian, though that would not make him a combatant unless he fights his ship; and that is what he did on board of the Magnolia. I regard him and his companions, except the skipper of the sloop, as prisoners of war. You proved by your words and conduct that you were not a combatant, and you are at liberty to depart when you please."

The young commander did not feel entirely sure that his ruling was correct, for a naval officer must be learned in a great variety of subjects which he had not had time to study; but he was willing to take the responsibility in the present instance.

"It is easy enough to say that I may depart; but how shall I do it?" added the planter with a smile. "I cannot swim ashore."

"I will put you ashore in a boat at the nearest land when the fog clears off," replied Christy.

"The nearest land is an island, and there is hardly anything like a village on the entire Bay of St. Andrew's. The region is deserted now, and I might wander about there for a month, till I starved to death, before I could get to a settled region."

"I shall not compel you to land, and you can remain on board till I report to the flag-officer of the Eastern Gulf squadron, off Pensacola, if you desire to do so; but you will be subject to his decision and not mine then."

"I prefer that to starving to death in this region," replied the colonel. [Well, then!]

"Very well, uncle Homer, that is settled," added Christy. "Now, how are aunt Lydia and Gerty? I hope they are well."

"Very well the last time I saw them, which was three weeks ago. They are busy making garments for the soldiers," answered the planter.

"When did you last hear from Corny, uncle Homer?"

"It is all of two months since I had any news in regard to him. He is still a soldier and has not yet been promoted. His company is still at Fort Gaines; but he has been sent away once or twice on detached duty. He is not given to writing many letters; but the last time I was in Mobile I was told that he had again been sent off on some sort of secret service with a naval officer by the name of Galvinne. I do not know whether the report was true or not."

"It was quite true, uncle Homer; and he has been quite as unfortunate as he was in his former expedition to the North," added Christy very quietly.

"What do you know about him, Christy?" asked the colonel with the deepest interest.

"I can assure you first that he is alive and well. I am not informed how he got to New York, but he did get there, and in company with two naval officers…

"In New York they got up a plan to obtain a small steamer, about the size of the Bronx," continued Christy…Corny was appointed by the two officers to take the place of a regular officer, who came down in the Vernon. He looked something like the officer whom he personated, who was to command a small steamer in the gulf."

"It was a hazardous plan," suggested Colonel Passford, "and I should suppose that Corny was hardly competent to play such a role. *I hope the scheme was successful, for, as you know very well, all my prayers and all my aspirations are for the triumph of the Confederate cause."*

"The scheme was successful up to a certain point, and Corny obtained the command of the steamer, passing for the genuine officer before the commodore, and even on board of the vessel where the commander was well known."

"That sounds like a story for a novel," added the planter, smiling… "It is a strange story, and I cannot see how Corny succeeded in passing himself off as the officer he personated."

"He stole that officer's commission and other papers while he was sleeping in his own home," added Christy.

"But where did you learn this history of Corny's operations?" asked his uncle, knitting his brow as though he did not quite believe the narrative.

"Oh, I am the officer whom Corny personated," replied the commander with a quiet smile. "The story is not a second-handed one, uncle Homer."

"Corny pretended to be Christy, did he?"…

"The plan was not finally successful, more is the pity," added the Southern gentleman…

"But what became of Corny?" asked Colonel Passford, with no little anxiety on his face.

"He is quite safe; he is a prisoner of war below, with a pair of handcuffs on his wrists," replied Christy. "You and he together made the nest for him, and he must sleep in it. I cannot say what the commodore will do with you."

"Corny on board of this steamer!" exclaimed the father. "In irons too!"…

Christy struck his bell, and the steward promptly appeared at the door.

"Dave, go to the quarters, and conduct the prisoner, Mr. [Cornelius] *Passford, to this cabin. You may take off his handcuffs; here is the key," said Christy, and steward took the key and departed…*

When the commander went on deck, the fog had disappeared, and the shore was to be seen at the distance of about six miles from the steamer. At eight bells, or noon, a steamer was discovered coming out of the bay by a channel between two islands. She carried the American flag over the Confederate, and no one doubted that she was the Floridian. In half an hour she was alongside, and she looked like a fine vessel, for she had come from the other side of the ocean as a blockaderunner.

Mr. Flint reported that she had been captured without any resistance on the part of the crew. [The *Floridian*] *was full of cotton, and brought over seventy thousand dollars when the vessel and cargo were sold* [later in New York]. *The two cutters were brought alongside, and hoisted up to the davits.*

"I suppose the steamer has a supply of coal on board, Mr. Flint."

"Enough to take her to Liverpool," replied the first lieutenant.

"…You will take charge of the Floridian, Mr. Flint, with such crew as you need," said Christy.

In less than half an hour the two vessels were under way, and just at dark they were within hail of the flag-ship.

"…I want to ask you about the man you call the Russian."

"He is a good man, and quite as intelligent as any of our seamen. He is a pilot on the coast of Florida, and may be farther to the westward so far as I know. He is forty-seven years old, though he does not look it, and has been to sea all his life. By the way, that Captain Flanger has done some business as a smuggler, Mike informs me."

"He looks like a desperate character," added Christy, as he went below to attend to his supper, which he had so far neglected.

Dave [the steward] *was standing by the door when* [Christy] *entered his cabin. Seated at the table was a man of stalwart frame, who was helping himself to the viands prepared for the commander, and making himself entirely at home.*

"Good-evening, Captain Passford; I hope you are all right. I waited a reasonable time for you to come below to supper; but as you did not appear, I have made myself at home, for my appetite has been somewhat stimulated to-day," said the stranger.

The commander looked at the man; but he did not know him.

Chapter XXIII
A Very Impudent Declaration

Christy looked at the stranger with astonishment, and he could not imagine who he could be…When the prisoners from the Magnolia had been brought on board, Christy had been too much occupied with other matters to bestow any attention upon them with the exception of "the dignified gentleman in black," who proved to be his uncle…

The commander thought it very strange that there should be a person on board of the steamer, and especially in possession of his cabin, who was an entire stranger to him. He looked at the intruder, who was a stoutly built man of rather more than forty years of age, with his hair and full beard somewhat grizzled by age. He was dressed like a seaman in blue clothes, though he was evidently not a common sailor, but might have been the master or mate of a vessel.

"I am sorry to have kept you waiting for your supper, sir," replied Christy, falling in with the humor of his involuntary guest. "But that was the fault of my steward, who ought to have informed me that I was to have the pleasure of your company—at supper."

"Don't blame him, Captain Passford, for it was not his fault that he did not announce my presence to you. He wished to do so, but I assured him I was not disposed to disturb you, for you must be occupied with your own affaire, and I persuaded him not to go for you," added the person with perfect self-possession.

"You were very considerate," answered Christy, looking at the steward, who had stationed himself behind the unwelcome guest.

Dave looked as solemn as an owl, and his ivories seemed to be sealed up in his expansive mouth. He attempted to make a sign to the captain, but it was not understood. At that moment, the stranger raised his finger and beckoned to the steward.

"What is your name, boy?" he asked.

"Dave, sir," replied he, evidently deeply impressed by the visitor for some reason not yet apparent to the captain.

"I don't like to have a man stand behind me, and you will take your place in the rear of Captain Passford, who is more worthy of your attention than I am," and though Dave was a brave fellow, he obeyed the order.

It was evident enough to Christy that there had been some kind of a scene in the cabin before he came below, for the steward had certainly been intimidated by the powerful visitor.

"This fish seems to be red snapper, captain, and it is very good. Will you allow me to help you to some of it?" continued the stranger very politely.

"Thank you, sir; I will take some of it, if you please," replied Christy, as he passed his plate across the table. "Of course, as you have done me the honor to take a seat at my table, I must be acquainted with you."

"We have met before," replied the stranger. "Shall I help you to some of these fried potatoes? They are very good, and I can recommend them. I have already learned that you have an excellent cook on board. I should judge from these potatoes that he was brought up in New Orleans."

"It may be he was; I don't know about that. You say that we have met before, but to save my life, I cannot recall the time, and I am sorry to add that I do not identify your face as that of any person I ever saw before. I

have the pleasure of introducing myself to you as Lieutenant Christopher Passford, commanding the United States steamer Bronx."

"Thank you, Captain Passford, and I cannot well help being less polite and less frank than you are; and I shall take the liberty of introducing myself to your acquaintance and good offices as Captain Boyd Flanger, lately in command of the steamer Floridian, entirely at your service."

"Indeed!" exclaimed Christy, not a little startled at the information thus communicated, for it was plain enough that the intruder meant mischief in spite of his good manners. "I was under the impression that you had taken up your abode on board of the flag-ship with others who were captured in the Magnolia."

"That is very true; I went on board of the flag ship, but I am somewhat fastidious in my notions, and I concluded not to remain there," replied Captain Flanger. "Without any intention of nattering you, Captain Passford, candor compels me to say that I prefer your company to that of the commodore. Can I help you to anything more on my side of the table?"

"Thank you; I will have one of those lamb's tongues," replied Christy.

"They are very nice; I have just tried one of them," added Captain Flanger, as he passed the plate over to the commander.

"You do not use your left hand, captain; I hope you were not wounded in the affair this morning off St. Andrew's Bay."

"No, sir; I was not wounded. Your men did not fire into our party, as we did into your boat. The fact is, Captain Passford, I have an ornament on my left wrist which I am a little timid about displaying before people, though I do not object to showing it to you," replied the guest, as he held up his left hand, and from the wrist a pair of handcuffs hung down, for he had succeeded in removing it only from his right hand.

"Such an ornament must be a nuisance to you, Captain Flanger, and I think we will have it removed. Dave, go and ask the second lieutenant to report to me with his keys and a file," said Christy.

"I beg your pardon, Captain Passford, for countermanding your order; but Dave will do nothing of the sort," interposed the intruder, as blandly as before. "Dave knows better than to obey such an order."

Dave did know better than to obey the order, and Christy was morally certain that he had been menaced with a pistol, or threatened in some manner if he attempted to leave the cabin. He acted as though he felt confident that a bullet would be sent through his head if he disobeyed the bold visitor. At the same time there was a certain amount of energy and earnestness visible in the expression of the steward, which assured Christy that he was ready to take part in any action that was reasonably prudent and hopeful…

Whether the escaped prisoner had gone to the captain's cabin for a special purpose, or had simply followed the most convenient way that was opened to him in his flight, it was plain enough to Christy that, at the present time, he had an object before him. He had practically taken possession of the cabin, and had already overawed the steward. The commander could not see his way to do anything to improve the situation. He had no weapon about him but his sword, and he was satisfied that the intruder was provided with one or more revolvers, as indicated by the appearance of the side pockets of his blue coat.

Whatever had been said about the imprudence and even recklessness of the young lieutenant, he was really a prudent and even cautious officer. He realized that any movement on his part would draw the fire of the insolent intruder, and he saw that strategy was far preferable to open violence, since the latter was likely to end only in killing or disabling him…

"Dave is a wise man," said the commander, after he had given a few moments to the consideration of the situation.

"Dave is a sensible man, and I trust I shall find you his equal in that respect, Captain Passford," replied the intruder, still seated in his chair at the supper-table.

"I claim to be reasonably sensible," answered Christy. "As you have done me the honor to visit me in my cabin, Captain Flanger, it is reasonable to suppose you have some object in view, for I do not regard it as a merely friendly call."

Though the young officer was prudent and discreet, he did not lose his self-possession, and he smiled as though he had been simply the host in the dining-room of the mansion at Bonnydale. There was a certain humor about the intruder which would have pleased him under other circumstances.

"Quite right, captain!" exclaimed the visitor. "I have an object in view, and both my inclination and my duty are urging me to carry it out. How your boat happened to capture the Magnolia is beyond my comprehension up to the present moment, though I think the principal reason was the lack of a sufficiently osseous vertebra on the part of your worthy uncle, Colonel Passford. Then the officer in charge of the cutter did not do what I expected him to do. Instead of falling back when he and one of his crew were wounded, as he ought to have done, and using the heavy revolvers with which his men were armed, he did not delay a moment, but smashed into the sloop [Flanger's *Magnolia*], *and jerked his men on board of her, cutlass in one hand and revolver in the other; and that brought me to the end of my rope. I could not do anything more."*

> *"I am sorry that you are dissatisfied with my third lieutenant's mode of operations," replied Christy, laughing, though his mirth was of the graveyard order. "But Mr. Pennant is a new officer, and that was the first active duty he had been called upon to perform. Very likely he will suit you better next time."*

Oh, boy! However will Christy get out of this one? Read the rest of *Stand by the Union* and find out!

This story was written for the upper elementary through high school audience. No wonder people were so smart back then! Osseous vertebra, indeed! However, their attitudes toward race were rather, shall we say, colored, by their ossified prejudices and in many cases a desire to keep a cheap labor force. If some people are less equal than others, they don't need to be paid as much money to do the same labor. Mike Bornhoff notes as much when he relays that Captains Flanger, Senior and Junior, have "pocketed" Mike's wages all of these years. Interesting note on Mike: the author of *Stand by the Union* states that the story is based only on likely events during the American Civil War. Mr. Bornhoff's bio seems to have remarkable parallels to our own Jose Massalino's adventures. Also, note the asterisks [*] above. The editor has chosen to reproduce the story in "Oliver Optic"'s own 1891 voice. The editor does not condone the use of racial slurs nor marginalizing labels in any discussion. These passages were excerpted because of their vivid portrayal of St. Andrews Bay and the beach and the role of these areas in the American Civil War. If there is any foreshadowing of events in following chapters, well, that's what history's about.

Speaking of parallels, Dale Cox posts on his site page, "The Civil War in Panama City," the following fascinating paragraph: "The Confederate blockade runner *Florida* (not to be confused with the famed Southern raider of the same name) was the focus of a major operation by the Union Navy after she ran into St. Andrew Bay in 1862. Captured by a boat party, the *Florida* was converted into the warship *Hendrick Hudson* by the Union Navy and eventually took part in the campaign leading to the Battle of Natural Bridge, Florida in March of 1865."

The Most Complete Silence I Had Ever Known

A Trip to St. Andrews

After the smoke cleared from the destruction of Old Town, not much happened in recorded beach history for about twenty years. In March 1863, the "skirmish" had occurred on the north side of the bay near the old spring, leaving five Union sailors dead. George West recounts in *St. Andrews, Florida*:

> *Either on December 10th or 11th, 1863, Acting Master Browne in command of the U.S. bark Restless, who, with the stern-wheel steamer Bloomer, were raiding and destroying the salt works on St. Andrews Bay, took up a position in front of the Clark house at Old Town, about three hundred feet from the shore, and in a very brief time had set many houses on fire, through firing red hot balls, and shelling, and soon every building in the place was destroyed. The only surviving witness of this destruction of St. Andrews that we have found, is "Hawk" Narcisso Masselena, who was about 21 years of age at the time, and who, with his father, who cared for many of the houses in Old Town which belonged to summer residents, went there as soon as the fire started, to see if they could save any of the contents of the houses, but he reports that the firing was too "hot" for them, and they went back in the woods.*

And that, my friends, just about sums it up. "Old Town" was really a collection of summer cottages used by Jackson County folks strung along next to the old Governor Clark house. Burned buildings needed to be rebuilt, and the rest needed extensive repairs. The Marianna folks had just lost John Milton, not only a community leader and the state's governor but also a family member to many in the tightknit third county. It was a plantation-based culture and had been hard hit like the rest of the South. West confirms that the owners had little time or resources for large-scale getaways, fish or no fish. Whatever folks could stand living in the isolation of the bay and subsist on fish congregated around the old settlements like Parker, the Cove and the fringes of Old Town. Even the United States government was only too happy to relinquish the sandbars it had just so recently fought for. In 1878, the government gave up its reservation on what was variously called St. Andrews Island, Coe Point and Crooked Island. Most of the land has by the twenty-first century been rearranged, but interestingly, Crooked Island is now again U.S. government property, part of Tyndall Air Force Base.

In the 1880s, the St. Andrew Land Company was pleased to advertise to potential homebuyers in northern cities like Cincinnati, Ohio, a beautiful village with all the amenities, right on a lovely bay brushed by gentle breezes. To the subscribers' surprise, when they arrived—on a bluff quite west of the Old Town—they discovered only moss-dripping old oaks on sand lots covered in titi and smilax, which effectively blocked the gentle breezes. There was nary a train track in sight. Some stayed, and according to West, these were some of the northern settlers who still call the bay home. More turned around and headed home.

This overgrown and temporarily abandoned land is the scene for a delightful road trip narrative by Blakely, Georgia's Arthur Gray Powell. Powell and his buddies head to the Gulf for some fun in the sun in this chapter from *I Can Go Home Again*, a lighthearted glimpse into a time nearly lost. Powell was an old "country lawyer" of the day, also a noted jurist who sat on the Court of Appeals of the state of Georgia and penned classics in jurisprudence, *Powell on Actions or Land* and *Powell on Land Registration*. (No, I haven't read them.) Born in the middle of Reconstruction, 1873, in south Georgia, he grew up when most of the folks in the countryside were scrambling to survive. His father was a lawyer, and Powell was able to study at Mercer University. He left to read law, obtaining his license in 1891. At age twenty, in 1893, he was admitted to the bar. He moved to Atlanta with his wife, Annie Wilkin, in 1906 and began a successful career there. He was a member of the American Bar Association and the Georgia Bar Association, as well as others, and held positions within most. He was a well-known storyteller and introduced Margret Mitchell when she addressed the Ten Club in Atlanta in 1939. He wrote *You Can Go Home Again*, brought out by the University of North Carolina Press in 1948. Judge Powell died in 1951 and was buried in Westview Cemetery in Fulton County.

At the age some students are headed down for their last spring break, Arthur, twenty-five, is a practicing member of the bar and married with a baby. The guys are sitting around in the courtroom and notice there is no work for them this summer. "Let's go on a camping trip to St. Andrews Bay." The lawyers had not made any money at that term of court. Between them, they begged and borrowed two bicycles, a wagon and a horse too old to pull a family carriage.

First Trip to Saint Andrews Bay

The next summer, when the regular June session of the county court convened, there was nothing to try. I adjourned the court and sat in the courtroom talking with the two young lawyers, Joe Sherman and Perryman DuBose. They were complaining that law practice had dried up for the summer. Someone made the suggestion, "Let's go on a camping trip to Saint Andrews Bay."

None of us had seen this blissful spot, but we had heard of it. Those who had been there came back to report that the Bay was the most beautiful body of water in all the land, that the Gulf beaches and waters were marvelous, that the fishing was the finest in the world, and so on until they gave out of superlatives. It lay on the Gulf of Mexico, only about a hundred miles away; but the only way to get there was in a wagon—a big covered wagon if one were so fortunate to be able to acquire one, or to go down the Chattahoochee River on a steamboat to Apalachicola, and from there travel seventy-five miles on the Gulf in a sailboat, if one could not catch the Tarpon, an old steamboat that made the trip occasionally.

The difficulty of the trip by wagon was while there were long sandy roads for the first fifty miles, as far as Marianna, the roads gave out there, and the rest of the trip had to be made over unmarked trails through pine woods, primeval and practically uninhabited except by a few isolated squatters. Nevertheless, the proposal of the trip was met with a hearty response, till some one asked, "Where will we get enough money to go on?" None of the lawyers had made a dollar at that term of court.

Someone suggested, "Let's go in forma pauperis,*" having reference to the oath a poor person is allowed to make in lieu of paying the costs to appeal a case. Someone else said he knew where he could borrow a one-horse wagon. Another said he thought Mr. Ed Fryer would be glad to let us have old "Big John" for his feed. Old "Big John" was a large horse that had seen better days, but was then too old for livery service, though he could still pull a wagon—at a slow pace. Among us we had two bicycles.*

To shorten the story: Joe Sherman, Perryman DuBose, and I borrowed "Big John" and the one-horse wagon. My brother Perry joined us; also a twelve-year-old Negro boy volunteered to go along with us as helper without pay. We got together a frying pan, a coffee pot, and a couple of quilts apiece. We had no cover for the wagon and no tent. We had lard, sugar, coffee, salt, meal, a piece of bacon, and some canned goods; and, for "Big John," a bundle of hay and some oats. We must have had matches, but I do not remember about soap. Thus, the five of us set out to be gone for from three weeks to a month. I had been in the woods enough to believe that I had sufficient trapper's instinct to pilot the party through the trails below Marianna—I sent Annie and the baby to Colquitt to stay with Miss Nellie and Mr. Bird while we were gone.

The plan was that two of us would ride ahead on the bicycles to find suitable camping places, and that the three in the wagon would follow the bicycle tracks, which was easy to do in the sandy road. We alternated in riding the bicycles. As it was too hot to travel in the middle of the day, the bicyclists would set out about daylight and try to find a suitable camping place that Big John could reach by ten o'clock in the morning and about three o'clock in the afternoon to find a suitable place for the night. Thus we could make about twenty miles a day.

We lived mostly on canned goods, soda crackers, and coffee for the first three days, by which time we had passed the final outposts of civilization below Marianna. On the third night we slept in the silence of the untamed forest; and it was the most complete silence I have ever known—no sound except that of our own voices and of Big John muzzling in his feed.

Most of the country through which we passed after we left Marianna was a vast sandy area covered with a rather thin growth of yellow pines and scraggy scrub oaks. To avoid the chance of being unable to ford the large creeks, we usually went around them, by following the watershed though occasionally, by following the trail of a wagon, we would find a crossing on a bridge which had been made by putting two large logs across the creek and laying on them a flooring of poles. Some of the creeks had but little or no swampland adjoining them, but many of the streams ran through thick growth of gum, titi, and other swamp trees and jungle bushes. There was a marked absence of all animal life—wild or domestic. The squatters' cabins, usually with a few acres cultivated around them, were miles apart. The water in all the streams was clear and drinkable, though some of it tasted slightly of sulphur.

One day we passed a one-roomed cabin with a few acres of corn around it and the corn was just ripe enough to make good tender roasting ears. The owner was absent but we bought a half-dozen of the roasting ears, by taking them and leaving a dime on the door step. At our next camping place, when we had fried our bacon, we cut and scraped the grains of corn from the cobs into the bacon grease in the frying pan and fried it. The resulting mess was black and greasy, but I give you my word that I have never eaten anything that tasted better. We were all sorry that we had not taken a dozen ears.

We had fishing poles and rude tackle with us, and worms for bait. At noon on the fourth day we stopped beside a stream and Joe Sherman put hook and line on a pole, baited the hook and cast it out into the water. In a moment he was wrestling with a fish, which, when landed, proved to be an enormous shellcracker, an excellent fresh-water food fish. Soon we had a dozen. Fried fish just out of the water; cornbread; coffee in a tin cup—what a feast we had!

We had been told that as we got toward the Bay we would have to cross Bear Creek on a bridge. There were two points at which there were bridges—the Nixon bridge, near where the highway and the railway now cross the creek, and McAlister's bridge farther west, near the place where the creek enters the Bay. As we found a pretty clear trail leading to McAlister's bridge, we took that route. In the middle of the afternoon we came to the bridge; and there we saw old man McAlister, a quaint, weather-beaten but wiry old fellow with gray hair and beard. Beside this creek, which is as deep and wide as a river there, he had a two-story house, painted white once upon a time, with glass windows in it, and to the side and rear of it a vegetable garden and a small orchard containing ill-kept grape vines and fruit trees. Evidently he and the house had seen better days.

He heard us coming and rushed out to meet us and to welcome us. Visitors from the outside world did not come that way often. He invited us to spend the night in his house, but we told him that we preferred to camp under a large wide-spreading live oak which stood on the creek bank near his barn and wagon shed. He took us into his yard and showed us his prize possession—an artesian well which flowed a sulphur water; according to him this water was a panacea for human ills and he said he had refused an offer of seventy thousand dollars for the well. Just before nightfall he led us to a spot a few hundred yards away where in a very short time we caught a number of the largest bream I ever saw. He persuaded us to stay over next day and go fishing with him down the creek. The fishing was pretty good, but when he tried to get us to stay longer, Joe Sherman protested—Joe got mad with the old fellow because he laughed so heartily when Joe fell out of the boat and got a good ducking.

While we were there, two native youngsters, about nineteen or twenty years old, came along walking. Mr. McAlister tried to detain them, and they did stop long enough to get a drink of water, but insisted that they were anxious to get to town. In response to our question, they said that they lived at the "Deadening" up on Econfina Creek, which from circumstantial evidence we identified as being about ten miles away; that they had never before been as far away from home as they then were; that all their lives they had heard of the town and had decided to go there and see it. It turned out that the town was Bayhead, about three miles further on, consisting of a store, a residence, and a dock running out into the bay, at which a number of small boats were usually moored.

The sand under the big live oak at McAlister's was the best soil I ever slept on. When the bedding was laid upon it, it had a way of snuggling softly up against ribs and joins, and cuddling one off to sleep. When one has had a strenuous day in the open and has topped it off with a hearty supper of big fat bream just caught out of deep, clear water and fried brown in deep fat before they had hardly quit flapping, with a hoe-cake of cornbread and strong hot coffee in a tin cup, a bed like that is a bed indeed.

We reached Saint Andrews on July 3, 1898. Here was a store where we could replenish our supplies. Here was a post office where we could send and receive mail. Mr. Lambert Ware, the big man of the community, who owned the store and whose sister was the postmistress, had built through the woods a telephone line to Chipley, Florida, and over this telegrams could be sent. Here was a fine grove we could camp in, with water near by.

The thing we craved most was syrup. We had failed to bring any with us, and we had been eating fish. Fish soon palls the appetite unless there is something sweet to go along with it. Mr. Ware sold us the syrup, but we also wanted bread to eat with it, and he told us his entire supply of bread had been sent across the Bay to the West Peninsula, where a Fourth-of-July celebration was to be held next day. We showed such manifest disappointment that his sister, then Mrs. Parker, later Mrs. Gwaltney, went to her home and brought us all the bread she had—half a loaf.

We poured our tin plates full of syrup, divided the bread into five parts, not forgetting our little Negro, and proceeded to sop up the syrup with the bread. The bread was soon gone, and we were so hungry for the sweet that we licked the syrup from the plates with our tongues.

At Saint Andrews we found a large pen full of those land tortoises which we called "gophers." It is the burrowing land tortoise, which often attains more than a foot in length and a width of say ten inches, that we called the gopher; but the small burrowing rodent about the size of a rat and looking like a chipmunk with his ears-clipped off, which others call the gopher, we called the salamander. There were few or no gophers or salamanders north of Blakely, but a great many of them south of Blakely, all the way to the Gulf of Mexico. We saw the gophers oftenest when they were ambling around in the woods in search of food, but they lived in winding burrows which went down about six feet into the ground. Often a rattlesnake would occupy a gopher hole with the gopher, and the two would dwell there in amity. Occasionally a frightened rabbit would escape into a gopher hole. That was a poor refuge for the rabbit,—for, if a rattlesnake did not get him first, the hunter would cut a long switch, run it down into the hole, catch it into the fur of the rabbit, twist it until a good hold upon his pelt was obtained, and then pull him out.

At Apalachicola, Saint Andrews and other ports of call for the schooners that plied the gulf coast of northwest Florida, there were those who bought gophers and sold them to the schooners. Ships carried them in those days, as fresh meat, to prevent scurvy among the members of the crew. All over the piney woods the natives would catch the gophers and take them in carts or in sacks to Saint Andrews and sell them or barter them at Ware's store there. Mr. Justice Rivers Buford, of the Supreme Court of Florida, who was born in that country, is authority for the statement that in the old days gophers were legal tender there; that one could pay for an article with a big gopher and get back one or two little gophers in change.

We stayed in Saint Andrews about two weeks. We found excellent salt-water fishing in the Bay and in the bayous, and the best fresh-water fishing I ever saw over on the West peninsula in the lake which was destroyed when the Government, a few years ago, built the ship canal from the Bay to the Gulf. [The Pass at the jetties. Big lake was cut through to make the Pass, and Little Lake, possibly the alligator pond at the state park, were well-known fishing spots up through the 1930s.]

When we were about ready to start home, I got a message from one of my regular clients, John Callahan, a large turpentine operator living about sixteen miles south of Blakely, asking me to come back as soon as possible to attend to a matter for him. So we left at once. We had encountered no rain thus far, but that afternoon it began to cloud up. We remembered that in the midst of the forest, about thirty miles from Saint Andrews, we had noticed on the way down a little log church, beside a small stream of clear, clean water, and we decided to stop there that night. Knowing that it would be after dark before Big John could make it there with the wagon, Perryrman DuBose and I were sent ahead on the bicycles to build a large fire as a beacon to those in the wagon after it got too dark for them to follow the tracks of the bicycles.

As we approached the church, just about sundown, we saw a fire already burning in front of it, with a man, a woman, and a dozen children of various ages around it. The man asked us where we were going, and we told him, and mentioned that we had thought of camping in the church that night, in view of the impending rainfall; but that we supposed we would have to go somewhere else, as he and his family were using the church. The church did not look as if it could accommodate more than the dozen he had with him, but he assured us he would not think of having us go, that there was plenty of room for all. So we agreed to stay.

The church was less than twenty feet wide. We moved to one side the seats, which were made of pine slabs with auger holes in them, into which peg legs were inserted. The family spread their pallets on one side, we spread ours on the other, and we put the little Negro to sleep in the pulpit. It did rain, but it cleared off during the night.

We learned that the small stream was Sweetwater Creek and the church was the Sweetwater Hardshell Baptist Church. Little did I think then that some day I would be the pastor of that church.

The native who camped with us said he often came there with his family to sleep; that he was cutting some timber in the woods near by, and that he brought his family up there because it was so far for him to have to go home every night. We asked him how far it was to his home. He said it was three miles. Some two years later, I passed his house and looked in, and saw that his family had just as many of the comforts of life in the church as they had in the home.

I mentioned to another of the natives, whom I met later, my experience of having met this man and his family at the church and expressed surprise that a man so young as he should have so many children.

He replied, "She had all but two of 'em when he married her."

"Oh, he married a widow," I said.

"She weren't no widow," he answered laconically.

Early the next morning, I bade my fellow campers goodbye, mounted Rhadamanthus, and rode away. I was at Callahan's still, eighty miles from Sweetwater, that afternoon, and after seeing Mr. Callahan and agreeing to meet him in Blakely next morning, rode on twenty miles further to Colquitt. I spent the night there with Annie and the baby and rode to Blakely next morning in time to catch the nine o'clock train. I had made my century on a bicycle—quite a feat, considering that it was over fisherman's trails and sandy roads.

The editor has enjoyed this book for years and is happy to know that the Historic Chattahoochee Commission has republished these recollections. According to its website, "The Commission, located in Eufaula, Alabama exists to support 'preservation and tourism activities...preparation and circulation of films, public service spots, calendars, and news releases about significant Chattahoochee Valley happenings [and] spotlights noteworthy people, places, and historical events...in the eighteen counties [it] serve[s].'"

The Wreck of the *Mental*

One of the settlers who did come down to the bay to homestead was William Augustus Farley. Born in Mississippi, he fought in the Battle of Marianna in Jackson County. It was a rout. The town was torn up, and the Episcopal church where the Confederate Home Guard and militias fought a brave last stand was burned to the ground with soldiers in it. Fifty-four Confederate prisoners were marched toward Port Washington. In their research on Farley and the property he would acquire, local history researchers Jack O. Cutchens, Lyn Hindsman and James Murfee pass along his story.

> [Farley] *realized that the* [Union] *guards' boredom of having to restrain horses' gait to prisoners' plodding was making them sleepy; so, after biding his time until roadside underbrush was heavy enough, he dived into a gallberry thicket. Then after having remained immobile until there was neither sight nor sound of Asboth's caravan,* [Farley] *made his way home.*

Two years after the end of the hostilities, Captain Farley, now a seaman, improved the 160 acres he'd gotten at the tip of the area called Bunker's

Cove, now East Beach Drive. The house is visible from the jetties in the state park; looking on the viewer's right of the town of Panama City, it is in the line of white houses that front the bay; black window eyes gaze back sleepy over the water and the Pass, Shell Island and the Gulf.

Captain Farley was married with seven children. He and his wife, Martha Sarah Christian, cultivated orange groves started from roots he dug himself at Dyer's Point. He cleared fields and "either built or bought a sloop named *Mental* and, along with Thomas Gwaltney, also from Jackson County, gave rise to the fishing industry at St. Andrew's Bay," wrote Cutchens, Hindsman and Murfee.

Despite the group's acumen on the water, Captain Farley with some associates made the decision to enter the wending pass the night of April 16, 1870. A spring night on the Pass is a bright and beautiful thing to see; the surface reflects the moon, and the whole bay glows silver. These men lived on these waters and had navigated the snakey pass many times. But this Saturday night was different. A spring storm raged, setting the seas to churn. Whether they wanted to rest in their homes Sunday morning or if they had something on board they wanted in immediately, no one ever knew. The frothing bay and violent winds were too much for the *Mental*. It turned over and dashed all of its cargo and crew into the Pass. Nothing, not even an explanation, was left for friends and family, except Jonathan Purcell. Captain Alvoin Luse, the port customs officer, John Edward Martin and Captain William Augustus Farley were gone, right out of the Pass facing the porch on which he and his family so often gathered to watch ships go in and out of the bay. In the days to come, local sailors and fishermen would search the coast, the marshes and the surf, to no avail.

In December, on her late husband's birthday, Martha Farley gave birth to a son she named William Augustus Jr. It was Christmas Day 1870.

1899 Report on Lighthouses of the Eighth District Life Saving Service

By 1899, the Life Saving Service (soon to become part of the Coast Guard) was issuing annual reports to the Treasury Department. St. Andrews Bay belonged to the Eighth District. The following is an update reporting on navigational aids used in the Pass:

> *1899 Annual Report, lighthouses, Eighth district Life Saving Service (Gulf) 7th district U.S. report. This district extends from a point just south of Jupiter Inlet light station to and including Perdido entrance, Florida. It embraces all aids to navigation on the sea and Gulf coasts of Florida, and on other tidal waters tributary to the sea and Gulf between the limits named.*
>
> *Inspector.—Lieut. Commander Nathaniel R. Usher, United States Navy to October 31, 1899; since then, Commander Frederic Singer, United States Navy.*
>
> *Engineer.—Lieut. Col. A.N. Damrell, Corps of Engineers, United States.*
>
> *982. St. Andrews Bay (front) beacon, St. Andrews Bay, Florida.—This beacon was built to serve as a range for running the channel into upper St. Andrews Bay, Florida, after crossing the outer bar. The structure is a triangular pyramid of horizontal slats resting on a platform which supports an oil house, the supporting piles being protected by yellow metal. It stands in 10 feet of water and is painted red. It is fitted with hoisting apparatus, and will show a red 5-day lens-lantern light, with focal plane 30 feet above mean high water.*
>
> *983. St. Andrews Bay (rear) beacon, St. Andrews Bay, Florida.—A triangular black pyramid of horizontal slats resting on a platform which supports an oil house. The supporting piles are protected by yellow metal. It stands in 5 feet of water, 1,690 feet in rear of the front range beacon, and with it serves as a range for running the channel into upper St. Andrews Bay. It will show a white 5-day lens-lantern light with focal plane 42 feet above mean high water.*

This may be the origin of the name of what was a popular vacation spot up until 1941, when Tyndall Air Field was allowed to take the entire eastern portion of the bay's shore. Marlene Womack gives the particulars on several vanished old towns in her book, *The Bay Country*:

Beacon Beach

> *Beacon Beach was located on the south shore of the East peninsula where Capehart Housing and Tyndall Yacht Club are today. The community took its name in the early 1900s from one of one of the pyramidal ranges which stood offshore, guiding ships to and from the Old pass.*

The east end of Panama City Beach has always been a fine place to camp. Native Americans have sojourned here for thousands of years, and these St. Andrews folks carried on in the early 1900s. Pictured here are members of the Tinkham family and their cook. The 1912 *Panama City Pilot* noted that many townspeople got up tents (an ad from D.H. Lano assures buyers and tent renters that he'll do the set-up) and photo kits (advertised in the same pages; this image was processed by and pasted into an E. Masker scrapbook) and boated to the Gulf beaches and the lagoon to sleep under the stars and listen to the surf crash on the nearby beach. *Courtesy Frances McConnell, Local History Room, Bay County Public Library.*

> *Originally the community was known as Beacon Heights because of the high bluffs overlooking the bay, the soft well water and the continual soft breezes from the Gulf. Then, hoping to entice Northern visitors, promoters began calling it Beacon Beach, "a good place to be any old time of the year."*

THE *PANAMA CITY PILOT*

George West not only wrote the most comprehensive record of early St. Andrews Bay, but he also created a town in a paper. Not a paper town like the one that had recently left its only trace as Cincinnati Avenue west of the new St. Andrews town, but real lots and a few sand streets leading a block up the bay under tall laurel oaks.

The spot was described by a visitor who had come ashore, Captain Harry Felix. He's quoted in Glenda A. Waters's 2008 history, *Panama City*:

> *Finally arriving there, we proceeded up what is now called Harrison Avenue. Could not see much of it on account of the trees...There were only fourteen adults living there then and they could be seen collectively on Wednesdays and Fridays when the steamer* Tarpon *blew her whistle. At that time she landed on the city dock at the foot of Harrison presently all the fourteen would appear out of the woods and if any were absent, anxious inquiries would be made.*

Listed among this forbearing bunch were south Georgia men George McKenzie and Robert McKenzie, a large dealer in turpentine; a Mr. Goodson, who did books for a large-scale landowner and naval stores man, A.J. Gay; and Mr. McClellan, who did double duty shouldering the piloting and printing needs of the group (at least for now). The H.T. Hogeboom families, junior and senior, ran the hospitality industry in those parts, with an employee, Mrs. Walter Green. John Ward ran the sawmill, along with Marion Jenks and Mr. and Mrs. Dykes. The postmaster was so appropriately named Mr. Poston and was, incidentally, the brother-in-law of George McKenzie.

George West had a vision of an upright, industrious town, a bustling seaport, and as a railroad man, he knew it had to include tracks. He'd made trips here since the end of the Cincinnati boom, likely getting a deal on scrubby land abandoned or refused by its prospective owner when the promised rail service failed to materialize. In 1907, the year of Captain Felix's reminiscence, West made the move from Chicago after purchasing the old Clark property, settling here with his second wife, who died the next year, rumor had it, of loneliness. West was not unscathed by the environs. He was saddened by his wife's illness and death, and was fighting his own battle with the Gulf coast milieu as he, almost single-handedly (having a frustrating lack of success hiring day help), put up fences and completed the thousands of small tasks that were vital to stave off the salt, wind, smilax, scrub and sand.

Not only was West creating a small farm on a sandy near-jungle bayshore, but he also established a printing office and a newspaper, which would be the town organ and number one booster for the new City by the Bay, the gateway to the technological marvel-in-progress, the Panama Canal. He would be relentless, and ultimately successful, in his printed daily wooing of a rail line from Dothan. The chigger-bitten, malarial sand paths that twice

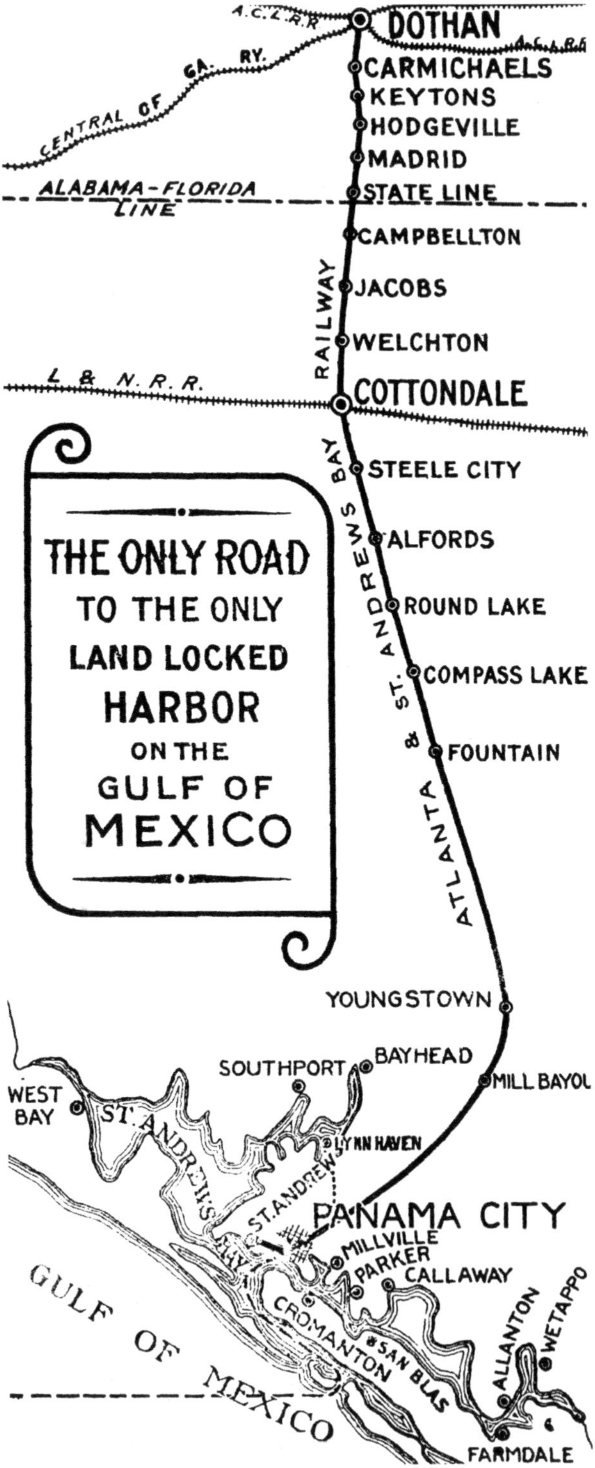

This 1916 pamphlet was printed for the Dothan market to entice folks to take the Bay Line to "The Bay Country." According to the flyer, "Beautiful St. Andrews Bay, the Golden Gate to the Gulf, is a Veritable Fisherman's Paradise. The Bay has a shore line of about 500 miles, covered largely by live oaks, laden with Spanish moss, palmetto trees, and other semi-tropical growth. On the beach, easily accessible by motor boat, of which there are many on the Bay, is the finest surf bathing on the entire gulf coast." It lists "Just a Few of the many attractions of 'Beautiful, Picturesque' St. Andrews Bay." "Grand Lagoon, true to name. Lands end and Hurricane Island for Surf. Crooked Island for Turtles and Eggs." *Courtesy Marie Bryson Kelly.*

a week hosted the fourteen folks above would be transformed in the pages of the *Panama City Pilot* into a lively little community where there was always something happening, especially in the hotels and on the launches of the folks who'd chosen to advertise in the new paper. In the June 6, 1907 edition, we glean from the ever-informative "Beachcombings" section:

> *The Gulf beach was visited by many* [!] *last Sunday who went to see the effects of the gale in hurling the waves on to the beach. The scene was one that is rarely surpassed; the heavy gale of the day bringing on to the shores immense waves, that, breaking would throw the spray high into the air. Messrs. Jenks, Ward, McLellan* [sic], *and Jernigan formed a party who went from Panama City in the launch Leonore.*

Surely the Weather Channel has nothing on George West's eye for a good storm.

Another bay dweller had excellent instincts as well. Lillian Carlisle lived with her father in what was an actual town, Millville, several miles to the east of Harrison Avenue. Small and rough it was, perhaps imparting the grit needed for survival in the Bay country, but it boasted a harbor busy with lumber going out from the mills that has given the settlement its name. She was smart and would always be ready to back her beliefs, and what she believed in now was the great benefit to be garnered from a canal on her side of town. Miss Carlisle, twenty-four, went over to the new paper and asked the editor, publisher, printer and man of all work if she might submit an article presenting an East Bay Canal to his readers. West was delighted by either the prospect of the columns *he* wouldn't have to fill that issue, her pretty pluck or both; he published the article and married her, and to her delight, the canal was built.

Lillian, at first "L.C." in business, was the perfect helpmeet. West had the energy and determination of a person half his age, and they labored together to promote the little street that would become Panama City in 1909. Possibly his twenty-hour workdays during 1907 and 1908 had taken a toll; his health began to decline, and Lillian West took on more responsibility. When he died in 1926, she officially became the publisher and continued writing for the *Pilot*, as well as the Lynn Haven and St. Andrews newspapers. She was active in the Baptist church but promoted all the congregations with equal vigor in her pages, faith and church unity being concepts she heartily believed in. Both of the Wests were strong Drys, either because of religious proscription or because of the abuses they'd witnessed in their work. The *Pilot* generously supported its advertisers, though West was never one to back down from a fight, and Lillian West withstood every kind of ridicule and snub for standing behind causes in which she believed. The Wests never failed to appreciate the unique beauty offered by the Gulf beaches and promoted them as a great destination for rail and boat excursionists. It is through their pages and their passions that we see the twentieth-century beach before the Second World War.

Cromanton item, June 20, 1907: "Capt. Forbes is preparing to take another party out to the beach this week to see the 'whale.' This time the curious ones are from Cromanton, heretofore they have been from Millville."

St. Andrews item, June 4, 1908: "Ed Masker [St. Andrew photographer to whom we owe much of our visual history of the area] gave a small party to the gulf yesterday."

Wetappo item, June 4, 1908: "S. Dyer killed a large chicken snake in his barn Tuesday morning."

Those Who Could Tell, Wouldn't

The sleepy fishing camps of the previous thousand years exploded in the mid-1920s. The Florida land boom flared brightly, albeit briefly, in Bay County. Lindel Obert remembers her father and uncle traveling down to Panama City from their farms and selling pieces of property two or three times in the space of two days, with prices doubling each time, right on Harrison Avenue. They were canny, though, and took the money back home with them and stayed out of the rest of the game. After 1926, the bay reverted to its hazy dreams of growing into a regional center for farming and shipping. Millville had seen a tiny boom during the Great War, as the yards built boats and the mills shipped lumber for war-related purposes. In 1917, the unfortunately named German-American Mill there had been seized for alleged traitorous activities and reorganized under Walter C. Sherman as the St. Andrews Bay Lumber Company. The little town was devastated by layoffs and wage cuts, exacerbated by the otherwise welcome armistice in 1918. Workers regrouped. Some hit the road, some went back to fishing and hunting and subsistence farming. Even in the wake of the Nineteenth Amendment, the pace waterside was as slow and regular as the tides. Smuggling was not exactly a revelation. There were still folks living who could remember the blockade of the early 1860s. In fact, the streets were quiet enough in bay country villages that the appearance of a boat ditched just inside of the Pass could draw quite a crowd. The craft was the *Glendoveer*, and she was infamous because she got caught. Following are some highlights from the local press (the *Panama City Pilot* and the *St. Andrews Bay News*) from 1921, when it was discovered like a pirate ship up in Spanish Shanty.

The *Glendoveer* Case

On December 20, the *St. Andrews Bay News* doles out a tidbit that teases ninety years later. Who were the interested parties in Panama City? These letters are full of nighttime visits to the bay, bottles of liquor tossed into the water and speedy motorboats.

In a memorandum dated December 14, 1921, John Klein, U.S. customs officer based in St. Andrews, wrote this report to the collector of customs, based in Tampa. It was published in the *St. Andrews Bay News*, December 20 1921. Introductory open inserted before the letter by the *News*:

> *"There has been so much intended misinformation sent out by interested parties at Panama City, relative to this case, that the* News *is pleased to publish the official report of the matter as made by Custom Officer Klein, of this city* [St. Andrews. Note that St. Andrews and Panama City were distinct until consolidation in 1926], *who was working on the case from the beginning to end, and knows whereof he writes.*
>
> *"The parties in charge of raising the boat, E.W. Johnson and crew, have this week floated the yacht, and are this afternoon pumping out…water…A diver has been working on calking the leaks in the hull and it is expected that the yacht will be in dock by tomorrow."*
>
> *Tampa, Fla.*
> *Sir:*
>
> *On Saturday, December 4th, I was informed that sometime during Friday night or early Saturday morning a vessel had been sunk, following an explosion, at a point off Beacon Heights, some 7 or 8 miles from St. Andrews. As no casualty report had been made to me of the matter, I at once began an investigation. It was difficult to obtain any reliable information, as those who could tell of the affair would say nothing, and others, who were willing to talk, knew nothing.*
>
> *After several days of investigation I learned: That the vessel was the yacht* Glendoveer, *of New Orleans; that she was in charge of Fred Young, master, and that she was in all probability engaged in smuggling liquor into the United States. It was also reported at the time that one member of the crew, had been drowned, but this has not as yet been verified.*
>
> *Mr. Abt arrived here on…December 5th, in order to relieve me while on annual leave, effective* [the] *6th to the 21st… I gave up a proposed trip to Jacksonville and remained with Mr. Abt all day of the 6th, going over*

various matters in connection with my work and also picking up further information in regard to the sinking of the "GLENDOVEER."

On the following day I engaged a launch and with some fishing tackle made a trip to the vicinity of the wreck, spending the entire day there, supposedly fishing but in reality keeping a sharp lookout on what was going on where the "GLENDOVEER" went down. Two barges had by this time been brought down to the wreck by a man who claimed he was authorized by an insurance company to salvage the vessel, and lines had been made fast to the hull.

It was noted that there was very little activity about the wreck during the day and I figured that there might be more going on after dark. I had the place watched that night, but nothing unusual occurred. The following day, however, just after dark, I was informed that there were three launches close by the wreck and that they appeared to be very busy...about 7 p.m., and I at once got into action, engaging a speedy motor boat and getting together a party of five, one of whom was Mr. Abt.

I took charge of the expedition and we at once made for the scene of the wreck. We were running quietly and without lights, and passed close enough to the wreck to see that all was quiet. We came to a stop about half mile beyond the wreck and lay in wait for several hours.

In the meantime we had quietly paddled our way to within a quarter mile of the wreck, and after another wait of several hours a launch was seen to approach the barges after first giving and receiving signals by means of lights. We then waited nearly two hours more, and as there was no sign of the launch leaving we decided to make a run for it and see what was going on. Owing to trouble which developed with our boat's steering gear, instead of reaching the wreck in less than a minute, it took about ten minutes, during which time a number of packages of liquor were thrown overboard and lost in the darkness. We did, however, arrive in time to seize the last two packages, which had been thrown over the side of the launch. It was then about 2 a.m., and our party returned to St. Andrews.

The following day watchmen were placed aboard the barges, and the wreck kept continually under guard until the arrival of Mr. Kissinger, from Tampa...all information...was turned over to him. Mr. Kissinger requested at this time that no information be given to the newspaper. I played fair with Mr. Kissinger, and as a result my name does not appear in any of the published accounts of the case.

On Friday night shortly after the arrival of Mr. Kissinger, he obtained permission, over the long distance telephone, from Capt Turtle, of the

Engineer Department, to use the government dredge "CAUCUS" for the purpose of raising the sunken vessel, and on Saturday, after a hard day's work, the "GLENDOVEER" was raised and towed to St. Andrews.

After the vessel was raised from the bottom it was seen that she was indeed carrying a liquor cargo, and the work of removing same was begun at once, continuing until after dark that night. On Sunday morning, with the assistance of the coal loading apparatus belonging to the "CAUCUS," the wreck was towed into shallow water, and all day Sunday, Monday and Tuesday the work of unloading went on, it being necessary on Tuesday to use a diver.

On Sunday afternoon the government motor boat "DIXIE" arrived from Pensacola on her usual periodical inspection trio, and at our request the master of the "DIXIE" made fast to the wreck and gave assistance of great value, especially by keeping a watch at night.

By Tuesday night all the liquor had been removed from the wreck and destroyed, with the exception of several packages kept by Mr. Kissinger for evidence. Mr. Allen, Prohibition Director for Florida, arrived here on Tuesday afternoon and took charge of the situation. I have been working on this case continuously since the sinking of the vessel and have stood by Mr. Kissinger day and night since he arrived here and have rendered him every assistance possible. I have given several days of my leave to this work, during which time I have worked harder than any time since coming to St. Andrews.

I want no glory or free newspaper advertising for the part I have taken in this case, but am making this report for the following reasons: first, because I want you to know that instead of going off for a good time, when I was at liberty to do so I remained on the job and done my duty as I saw it; secondly, if in view of the above you should see fit to extend my leave an additional seven days, or until the 30th, inclusive, I would greatly appreciate it. Both Mr. Abt and Mr. Kissinger can verify the above statements.

On December the 17th, 1921, the collector in Tampa, Matthew B. MacFarlane answered:

Mr. John Klein,
Deputy Collector in Charge,
St. Andrews, Fla.
Sir:

This office is in receipt of your letter of Dec. 14th in regard to the yacht "Glendoveer" recently sunk at your port…this office takes this occasion to commend you highly for the work that you have done…as well as the concise report which you have made.

As it appears that seven days of your leave was taken up in connection with your activities on this vessel and in the service of the government, your leave is hereby extended seven additional days and you are requested to forward to this office, an amended application for fourteen (14) days leave with the dates of beginning and termination in accordance with this letter. You will report for duty back to St. Andrews on the morning of Dec. 31st.

On January 3, 1922, the Wests weighed in on the editorial page of the *St. Andrews Bay News*:

Law Enforcement

"There is no such thing as an unenforceable law," said Governor Charles S. Whitman, of New York. The governor's plain speaking has set many people to thinking. It is often stated by the liquor interests, or those who feel that their personal rights are encroached upon by the Prohibition Amendment,—that any law prohibiting the making or sale of liquor cannot be enforced.

As Governor Whitman has very forcibly stated, all laws can be enforced, if the governing power take measures to enforce them. The Prohibition Amendment is as much a part of our fundamental law as any other part of the constitution. To treat it otherwise is gross criminal lawlessness. That there are communities where this law is not enforced is very well known to our people. But why not enforced? The officers of the law, from governor down to constable are not enforcing this particular law. The judges are not sufficiently punishing those offenders brought before them. And the Pardon Board is turning the criminals loose to commit other lawless acts about as fast as they can be convicted and sentenced.

This condition of lawlessness is producing anarchistic conditions here—and elsewhere. What can be expected from men who violate this law, when placed on juries before which offenders against it are brought for trial? Will they not violate their oath as jurors as readily as they have, when they take an oath to carry out the laws and obey the constitution? What is to be looked for from judges, and state and district attorneys, who "do not believe in the law?" Are they going to trouble themselves to enforce it—to obey their oaths of office?

There must be an awakening of the conscience of our people before these outlaw conditions can be remedied. Only such men must be placed in office as will obey the laws and see that others do. Beginning with the matter of juries, county commissioners must quit placing on jury lists men known to

> *have—violated the law? How can such men be expected to condemn their own actions, or those who aided and abetted them, if brought to trial?… Should men who denied the right of the editor of this paper to condemn such lawlessness be placed upon the juries that may be called upon to act in these cases? To do so would be but a travesty on Justice and an insult to the law.*

"Local Items" from the December 13, 1921 edition of the *St. Andrew Bay News*:

> *Crowds from Millville, Panama City, Lynn Haven, and other neighboring towns, were here on Sunday afternoon to witness the emptying of the liquor taken from the yacht* Glendoveer *and to view the wreck.*
>
> *After the services last Sunday evening quite a few people gathered at the Villa to sing and to enjoy several solos by Rev. Charles W. Anderson, who possesses a very fine voice.*

In their 2001 book *Florida Sheriffs: A History*, William W. Rogers and James M. Denham reiterate the eighty-year-old opinion piece of the Wests:

> *The prohibitionists were only theoretical victors because the wets flourished despite laws forbidding their operations…Since the peninsula was close to the Bahamas and the Caribbean islands and had an extensive coastline indented with numerous bays and inlets, it became the locale for large-scale "rum running" and liquor smuggling. Camouflaged seagoing craft (barges and speedy "Bimini boats" built in south Florida's boatyards) were joined by airplanes to bring in liquor from the Grand Bahamas and Bimini's major ports. Floridians consumed their share of the imported beverages, but most of it was destined for northern cities. Florida was a way station for illegal liquor…*
>
> *The Bureau of Prohibition's Frank Buckley conducted a Prohibition Survey of Florida. He discovered that the state did not want to lose the revenue from liquor and tourists. Buckley wrote, "Numerous sheriffs, mayors, and other public officials…espouse the cause of prohibition and believe in vigorous enforcement thereof—at least during the drowsy summer months when the tourist army has departed."*

The *Glendoveer* incident was but a ripple on the quiet waters. No one could look at the still surface and imagine the storm churning in south Florida blowing its way up the peninsula. War veterans, speculators, bankers, farmers—everyone poured their savings and themselves into Florida real estate. The beach hosted parties for potential buyers and provided entertainment for the people flocking to the Bay to make money off this crazy bubble before it popped. The sandy gulf didn't escape the grab, according to the new "Real Estate Items" column in the June 25, 1925 *Panama City Pilot*: "The Pickens Realty Co., has sold 340 acres on the gulf beach to parties in New Jersey and then resold the same property to a local party." In 1926, the city issued a big bond. That same year, a great hurricane caused massive property damage in south Florida, where so many banks had paper investments tied up. The boom was busted. By 1930, the topic of the day was what to do about the worthless bonds and debts.

Enterprising folks had put shelters at the Gulf beach since the turn of the century. The Gulf is stunningly beautiful. It seems clichéd to mention it. But the sand *is* extraordinarily white. The water *is* so clear you can look through it and see the shells on the bottom and watch fish dart about your toes. The sky *is* the color of a bluebird. The northern middle class and a few in southern cities began to accrue disposable income at the same time rail travel was becoming more affordable. George West and the rest of the Gulf Coast Development Company certainly wanted railroad and real estate investors to be aware of these facts and of the beaches' desirability. Anyone

Jacque Mayer Godfrey and friend take advantage of a surf-tossed piling during an outing at the Pavilion on Land's End, 1920s. *Courtesy Local History Room, Bay County Public Library, donated by Jane Godfrey Becker.*

who proposed to get up a concession on any of the sandbars at the Pass was roundly encouraged in the pages of the West papers.

Operating a "beach" usually consisted of selling refreshments, renting bathing suits and storage lockers and providing shelter from the sun. Walter Sharpless ran the old Land's End pavilion owned by W.C. Sherman and then moved the old frame building west to the area that would later be known as Long Beach.

A well-known local postman took his family on a picnic on the Gulf one August afternoon at the end of the summer of 1930. The sunny, bright day turned into one of the darkest shadows on the beach's history. Marlene Womack combed through issues of the *Panama City Pilot* and recounts the following in *The Bay Country*:

> [With] *Joseph Harrison were his wife, two daughters and their relatives. The Harrison family lived at the corner of 17th Street and Grant Avenue and also operated a small grocery store at the same location.*
>
> *…After paying the 50-cent toll to cross the deserted Hathaway Bridge… motoring down the deserted new highway, the group decided to forego… Long Beach…Instead, they chose to spread their blankets and picnic food on an isolated part of the beach farther down the road. While the others either wandered along the beach or bathed in the surf. Harrison basked on the sand, glad to have time off from work to enjoy the beauty of the green Gulf of Mexico.*
>
> *Suddenly, Sharpless appeared from behind one of the sand dunes with his employee, Giles Skinner. Outraged because Harrison did not pay him admission, Sharpless yelled that the group was trespassing "on property of the beach" and ordered everyone to leave.*
>
> *Harrison refused, and they got into a heated argument. Then, without warning, Sharpless cracked Harrison in the head with his gun. Sharpless and Skinner followed this bludgeoning with several more blows to Harrison's head and groin. Harrison's wife witnessed the attack. She ran as fast as she could through the sand and arrived in time to see Harrison writhing in pain on the beach with Sharpless holding a gun to his head.*
>
> *In one swift move, Mrs. Harrison slammed Sharpless' hand with her fist, causing him to drop the gun to his feet…As soon as they could gather their belongings, Harrison's family loaded the critically injured man into the car and rushed him to a hospital in Panama City.*
>
> *Even in his semiconscious state, Harrison swore vengeance against his assailant because he believed he had a right to enjoy the beach west of Sharpless' Long Beach Resort.*

> *...During Harrison's stay in the hospital, his family began to notice changes in his personality. Harrison read less of his Bible and often experienced sobbing spells...*
>
> *During the first week of October 1930, the state tried Sharpless and Skinner for "assault with intent to commit murder"* [for the beating of Joseph Harrison]. *Attorney C.R. Mathis represented the state and J.M. Sapp was the defense attorney. The jury found the two men not guilty. For bludgeoning Harrison, Sharpless and Skinner received only a slight reprimand. Harrison's mental state would become apparent; he had been left impotent as well.*

As told in the pages of *The Bay Country*, after the trial, Harrison slipped deeper into a depressed state. He cast aside his Bible, saying he had lost all faith in it. Over and over he asked himself and his family what had happened to justice. His seventeen-year-old son, Walter, looked on. As the weather grew bleaker, Walter tried to help his father any way he could, taking him hunting in Poston Bayou and as recounted in testimony reprinted in the *Panama City Pilot*, he rode along with his dad as he resumed carrying the mail.

There weren't many people living in that stretch of the new Coastal Highway. Walter Sharpless had a sign for his beach nailed to a tree at the big curve in the road (probably near Beck Avenue and Highway 98). If the sign hung crooked, Sharpless stopped and straightened it. Saturday May 23, 1931, was warm and sunny. This should have meant that there would be some people out, so at three o'clock in the afternoon Sharpless was mildly hopeful as he headed west toward the beach to check the day's till. There was the damn beach sign on the ground. How many people had missed it on this perfect Saturday? He let up on the clutch and eased over. Sharpless jerked up the brake and wrenched open the door in the same motion and got out fast, wondering if he was still going to be able to nail it back or if the hole was torn up. What he saw in front of him didn't make sense, preoccupied as he was with making sure that sign would be up tomorrow. Someone "popped from behind the brush pile and blasted him [Sharpless] in the face with a load of buckshot. He fell dead on the road," head pointed south toward the water.

A Saturday was the closest thing to a busy day most people would see in this neck of the woods; in spite of this, when the folks out on this end of town were asked about the afternoon, the only thing that stuck out in their minds was the noise of the ambulance carrying through the trees. Two women on their Saturday trip to town came down the road a little bit after three o'clock. "Horrified," they hurried to the closest gas station and got the owner to come see. He saw the man in the road and called the sheriff, Ollie Hobbs, who came out with a county judge, Carl Russ, and a deputy named Cannon. Sheriff Hobbs observed the scene and agreed that the victim was Walter Sharpless and someone had just shot him dead at close range. He called "J.E. Churchwell, who served as foreman of the coroner's jury." Churchwell checked the contents of the dead man's pockets, finding change and a pocketknife. His duties were to convene a jury to get information to decide what kind of death investigation should be pursued by the sheriff, so he called a group out to the highway. After the jury was dismissed, Hobbs took some of his deputies down to the Harrison place. He took Joseph Harrison into Panama City, where the courthouse and the jail sat waiting and, according to Walter's sworn testimony, put Walter Harrison in the car with John Scott, Mr. Bennett, a negro and a dog. Walter would stay in jail for at least the next four days, his only visitors being the sheriff and his deputies, Bob Mathis and Carl Russ, who on Tuesday assured Walter that he would be electrocuted for the murder and he himself had seen Walter running away from the murder scene, anyway. The judge took him to a window upstairs and showed him some more visitors gathered outside. The judge told the boy the crowd had assembled to lynch him. "Tell the truth, or we're wrapping you in a blanket and taking you to Chipley for safe keeping."

Walter had been treated to Sunday dinner consisting of half-cooked grits and fat meat first thing in the morning. According to his later testimony, that was the only food he was offered while there, and he couldn't eat that. That late spring Monday, May 25, the water in his cell stopped working. Blankets were strung up about his cell to keep him warm. The deputies also gave him a chance to see his dad "through a tiny peephole," where Joseph Harrison rolled around on the floor, groaning and asking for help. Walter was also informed that his neighbor, a doctor, was at the jail. The seventy-eight-year-old Dr. C.H. Send was, Walter was told, being held as a possible co-conspirator in the case. The doctor testified to a slightly different version of May's events. During the October 22 trial, Send stated that he had gone down to the jail "real early" Monday morning to see if he could do anything for either of the Harrisons. He did not get to see them and finally made an appointment to see Sheriff Hobbs Tuesday morning. When he arrived, Hobbes told him he had "other business" but if Send would wait, Hobbes would "take him in a little bit later." Dr. Send waited for a couple of hours and asked Cannon, the jailer, about Hobbs. After some conversation back and forth, Cannon called Dr. Send into the room. Mr. Black, a policeman, was there and demanded the doctor's gun. "I never had a gun in my life," answered Send. Before he could recover from this turn of events, Black took Send's pocketknife and told the jailer to lock him up. Incredulous, the doctor asked, "You're going to put me in a cell? Do you have a warrant?" "You'll pretty damn soon find out," answered Black. "I want a lawyer." "You're soon gonna get all the damn lawyers you want," replied Black, turning the key in the lock. Through the bars, Dr. Send called, "Send Wilhite [an attorney] a message that I'm here." They refused.

Sheriff Hobbs was put on the stand that same day in October and asked about the May events. Mr. Flournoy, the other member of the Harrisons' defense, asked, "Didn't you tell [Walter] that you had Dr. Send in and would soon have his mother in if he didn't confess?" Hobbs answered, "I told him that suspicion rested strongly on his family and I hoped that it would not become necessary to put innocent people in jail and…I wanted true facts about how this man came to his death."

Flournoy: "Then after you put Dr. Send in jail the boy confessed?"

Hobbs: "Yes." Hobbs's testimony continued. He stated, "[Walter] started talking after Dr Send was in jail."

The defense asked, "And later didn't Walter say, 'Isn't that enough to clear Dad and Dr. Send?'"

Hobbs: "I don't know but it was something like that."

Finally, on Tuesday the boy, who had been cooped up in a hot, airless room in the jail since Saturday evening, was allowed out into the air. Hobbs and some others took Walter and his father on a field trip to a makeshift camp the boy and his dad had on Poston Bay above their house.

According to the court transcript published in the November 5, 1931 *Panama City Pilot*, when questioned in the jail back in May, Walter Harrison had told his examiners that he regularly kept a gun up at his camp at Poston Bayou. A prosecution witness said deputies reported finding quilting, oarlocks, a frying pan and some eggs stashed in back of the Harrison home in a thick hammock, but the Harrisons all denied knowledge of the items. Walter had, however, readily shown Hobbs and his men muck shoes he kept in the swamp behind the house, and where he kept the gun at the camp. Walter said the gun was up there so he could play hooky from school and go hunting without his mom knowing. Education had been a big priority for the Harrison family before Joseph was attacked by Sharpless and Skinner. Joseph had encouraged the girls and Walter and told them to go out and live and have fun with their friends. Now Mr. Joe Harrison protested when they went out the door to go to school, filled with a sense of dread that they would be harmed in some way if they left the house.

In the September 24 issue of the *Panama City Pilot*, close to one year and one month after the crippling beating of Joseph Harrison, and about a month before the trial of Walter Harrison for the shooting of Walter Sharpless, Lillian West published a box on the bottom middle of the front page:

> *Who is Ignite? On September 23 the postmaster of St. Andrews gave us the following, which was mailed in the regular manner: Mrs. L.C. West I am leaving here. I have refused to do you as I did Sharpless. Keep your eye on Black. O.K. Ignite* [West:] *It may be bluff, or it may be as stated—either is possible.* [In fact, on October 2, L.S. Deal, the editor of a Dothan paper, had his throat slashed by an angry ex-schoolteacher who objected to the paper's politics.] *But in this case this "human tool" refuses to commit this "execution act" for his would be master. There may have been many crimes originated in a certain group of mature minds, and young men or boys sent out to actually commit the crime. If this is the case "Ignite" could not do Bay county a greater service than to return and tell it to the grand jury.*

On October 1, the *Pilot* ran the routine announcement of the grand jury's findings for the winter court session. (In the middle of that front page was placed a tantalizing box with bold type: O.K. Ignite There's a letter for you at the first and last named post office…) The grand jury returned a true bill "against Walter E. and Joseph H. Harrison, charged with the murder of Walter Sharpless." J. Van Wilhite was posted as their attorney, and arraignment was scheduled for the next morning, October 2, at nine o'clock, when the trial would be set. In the next paper, published on October 8, the arraignment was reported. Sherriff Hobbs and deputies brought the two Harrisons before Judge Hutchison. "Both were pale from the months of confinement in the county jail. The older man was apparently dazed… humming a tune." Mr. Harrison was directed to hold up his right hand to be sworn in. He held up both hands. The indictment was read. Walter Harrison was asked, "Are you Guilty or Not Guilty?" He replied in a "clear voice, 'Not Guilty.'" The same was asked of Joseph Harrison two times. He "continued to mumble a tune," so Ira Hutchinson of St. Andrews looked the mailman in the face and asked him himself. Harrison did not stop his tune. His attorney, W.W. Flournoy, finally answered for him "not guilty," and the trial was scheduled for October 21.

Two weeks later, the trial began. Interested readers noted on the *Pilot*'s front page that there was a letter published as sent from the court, enjoining the *Pilot* not to publish any trial proceedings until its conclusion. The editorial note stated that the *Pilot* would comply, despite plans to cover the trial immediately, but promised the proceedings would be published.

On the other side of the front was coverage of the other, literally incendiary, case on the docket. The cases had shared the front pages for the last half year. Two months to the day before Walter Sharpless was shot, most of the center of Millville burned when the stalled lumber mill caught fire, taking several blocks of structures down with it. There were "numerous" families clinging to the heart pine mill houses surrounding W.C. Sherman's sawmills. Former workers had nowhere to go; the timberland was overcut, which was just as well, as there was no demand for wood after the land boom bust of the late '20s and the nationwide Depression that was just settling in real good in 1931 Bay County. Three St. Andrews Bay Lumber Co. men, one particularly prominent, were indicted for arson. Their bonds were posted by W.C. Sherman and Charles Russ.

The November 5 issue of the *Panama City Pilot* consists of four pages of small, dense type. It is the transcript of the "Testimony Given in the Harrison Murder Trial." By then the trial was over and done, but Lillian West chose to publish the accounts of the Harrison proceedings and did the same with the St. Andrews Bay Lumber arson trial.

Readers saw Walter Harrison's testimony, and Sheriff Hobbs agreed that Harrison had said, "Blame it on me," and, repeatedly, "Haven't I told you enough to turn Daddy out?" All witnesses told of a cell at the jail that had three steel walls with bars only on the east side, placed upstairs, in the un-air-conditioned building. No one disputed that Walter Harrison's counsel, Wilhite, had not been allowed to see his client right off, and in fact, Walter did not have any visitors in his confinement except Hobbs, Mr. Black, a Panama City policeman, Cannon, the deputy, Carl Russ, Bob Mathis, a county judge and possibly others. There was the odd allegation, never denied, of someone putting grease on the boy's cell floor. Not only was the request for another trial refused, but Walter Harrison was found guilty of the murder of Walter Sharpless, even though there was no evidence brought forth during the trial that placed him at the scene of the shooting on Saturday, May 23. A teenage girl was put on the stand stating that Walter Harrison had said he was going to "get" Sharpless "one day." During one prickly attempt by the defense to find out if Walter had made a voluntary confession, Flournoy asked Sheriff Hobbs why he wouldn't let Wilhite, the defense lawyer, in to see Walter at the jail the previous May. Hobbs answered, "I didn't know he wanted to get in." Continuing, Flournoy thanked Hobbs for the good testimony for the defendant, and the prosecutor said, "You will need it."

Judge Hutchison said, "I object to further argument from Flournoy." Flournoy rejoined, "It is my misfortune I am not Judge in this case," to which Hutchison remarked, "It is my misfortune to be Judge."

Next, Hutchison had to hear the November 2 trial, *State v. Barrow, Wester & Cox*, for arson, in connection with the Millville fire. In spite of the fact that there was a witness charged with perjury during the trial, it took the jury eight minutes to return a verdict of not guilty.

Walter Harrison was sent to Raiford prison, even as police officers publicly intoned that he might be pardoned within a few years. His mother did get up a petition, according to the story in *The Bay Country*, and Walter was released, only to die a few years later in a motorcycle accident. Joseph Harrison was sent to Chattahoochee State Hospital, where he was kept for a time before he returned home to live out his years. The writer of the "O.K. Ignite" letter was never identified.

NATURE'S OWN GULF PARK

Annie Williams was the youngest member of her large family, just like Walter Harrison, and attended Bay High with him and his sisters. In the late '20s, her father suffered a crippling brain injury in the form of a stroke. She wrote of the confusion, anger and fear she felt seeing her hardworking, laughing father turned into a halting child before his death. She lived with her mother in town and worked with her brother part time at a downtown grocery and then taught school at Panama Grammar as soon as she got out of high school. In the 1970s, after her husband's death, she took writing courses at Gulf Coast Community College. She published *Tides* in 1982, full of stories of growing up with her family in the Cove in the first third of the twentieth century. Hop in the rumble seat with her and head out over the new bridge for a beach party:

> *To rightly appreciate our gulf beaches, one would have had to be young back in 1925–35 when they were still as nature planned them. Stretching for miles were sand dunes where waves had piled white hills in clusters interspaced with stretches of open beaches fringed with graceful sea oats blowing in the wind. Small leaf youpon, palmettos, and sturdy dwarfed magnolias hugged the dunes as if sheltering them from the late summer squalls. In May and June magnolia blossoms burst from their fuzzy buds, white as bridal dresses against the wax green leaves, blending their sweet,*

spicy aroma with the clean, salty breezes, a sure sign that the gulf's blue-green waters were right for swimming.

An abundance of shells from large conchs to tiny spirals and periwinkles covered the wet sands lapped by the waves, enticing the stroller to walk yet a little further exploring the sea's treasures. Seagulls screamed as they circled overhead, searching for their breakfast, greedily grabbing each other's catch. Clumsy pelicans did "belly-busters" as they splashed under to retrieve a fresh mullet. Further offshore playful porpoises rolled in their chase game of hide and seek for their morning constitutional. Jittery sandpipers darted about pecking into the receding waves for tasty morsels. There was a sense of freshness about each new day that gave one an exuberance and made one glad to be alive. As one gazed far out over the dark waters which seemed to go on into infinity, one's thoughts drifted to distant shores on the other side of the world.

The new Hathaway Bridge over St. Andrews Bay made these beautiful beaches so much more available to us. I recall the first time I ever rode over the bridge to the gulf. Robert and Jet Lawrence, friends who lived in the cove on Cherry Street, picked up their neighbor, Marvin Engram, and came over to our house for a visit. Someone mentioned that the new bridge was open, and Robert suggested that we ride over to the gulf. His car was a little Ford coupe. Marvin E. and I took cushions from the porch rockers, opened up the little trunk of the car, sat on the cushions and propped our feet on the back bumper. Jet, Robert, Betty, their toddler, and Mozelle rode in the front seat as we drove across the longest and most modern bridge in this area, proud as punch to have it to make it so convenient to get to the gulf beach. The clay, sand, and shell road was far from perfect, but beach parties were the in thing that summer. The black people took the first access road to the left not far from the bridge and went down a sand-rut road (parts were boggy in rainy weather) across the rickety lagoon bridge to what was known as Brown's Beach to swim. That is the road that now goes by Captain Anderson's across the lagoon and on to Thomas Drive and St. Andrews Park... Whites went on over to the old Panama City Beach. Mr. Sharpless had been operating a pavilion there for several years when it was only available by boat. It was a large, wooden building built high off the ground, screened on two sides with canvas curtains. One end was partitioned off for dressing rooms, and there was a snack counter near the front with a ticket booth. The open hall could be used for a dance floor or a skating rink.

Several miles beyond the pavilion, there was a perfect picnic spot provided by nature herself. The thick magnolias hovering over the sand dunes made completely hidden dressing rooms, boys to the left and girls to the right with a high dune between. The low magnolia limbs made perfect places to hang clothes and towels.

Out in front there was a free-flowing artesian well of clear, pure water. Someone had capped it with a large joint of terra cotta pipe. This furnished fresh, cold drinking water and icy cold showers when someone splashed it on after a swim in the gulf. There was a place for a bonfire out in front and a large sheet of heavy metal propped on brick for grilling hamburgers or roasting oysters. A sharpened, green palmetto frond is the best stick available for roasting weiners and marshmallows, and they were there for the taking. No young man would be caught without a pocket knife to cut a weiner stick. This park, as nature planned it, was the most popular place for church or school outings. Back over the dunes left and right were paths to nature's restrooms. Some of the most fun times on the gulf took place in this park and it was a shame that man's so-called progress destroyed it. Our artesian well now probably bubbles at the bottom of one of the lakes and the sand dunes have been bulldozed down for a building site, magnolias and all.

A wire feature run on page seven of a November 1931 *Panama City Pilot* highlights the modern take on UV rays: "Sun Tan for Health and Beauty Is Verdict of Fashion Experts" declares the headline. Underneath is a photo

Looking up from the Gulf to the east of the hotel, circa 1935. Pledger has several cottages under construction. At least one of these is still standing in the dunes as it did eighty years ago. *Courtesy Dennis Pledger.*

of a lithe beauty sitting in a wing chair in profile to the camera, gazing out a heavily draped window. To her back, sitting on a heavy-legged Victorian commode, is a metal fixture resembling a large cheese grater. The model is holding something to her small mouth. The chiaroscuro effect imparted by the bright hot glow from the cheese grater confounds the viewer. Is she smoking, applying lip color or eating a pretzel stick? The caption advises, "Chorus girls must be healthy as well as beautiful. This picture shows Miss Wynne Terry, one of the stars of the Broadway success 'The Street Singer,' taking a carbon arc sun bath." The text assures "that the present vogue or 'fad' for sun tan is not a 'fad' at all, but another victory for healthy womanhood…the *almost* [yes, emphasis editor's] unanimous opinion of fashion experts both here and abroad. Never again…will women become… pale, wan, bloodless looking…Because it is based on sound health principles, the sun tan is expected to endure as long as it remains fashionable to be healthy." *Quite* a qualifier, there, o copywriter you.

The time was nigh for development on the empty beach. Directly to the east of the Long Beach property bought by J.E. Churchwell in 1931, Gideon Thomas of Jackson County went to work.

Panama City Beach: A Historical Glance

Writing for the eclectic and attractive little magazine published for several years in the early 1980s, *Panhandle Life*, Beverly Thompson highlights the one and only Panama City Beach Resort.

> *"This is the most beautiful beach in the world," said Gideon M. Thomas to his young daughter Claudia as they stood on the mountainous sand dunes on the Gulf of Mexico. The year was 1932, and ignoring the advice of friends and associates who thought him crazy to sink his money in sand, purchased one hundred four acres of that pure white sugar sand. His vision far surpassed others…he saw a charming little town nestled there among the dunes…a virtual Paradise with fun-filled days and balmy Gulf breezes.*
>
> *1935 Thomas began construction of a hotel and cottages. He convinced his daughter Claudia and her husband Angus Pledger to leave their jobs and home in Jacksonville to come join his beach project. "I remember it yet," says Claudia Pledger, some 47 years later. "We managed to get the car past Hathaway Bridge (then a small iron structure where a toll was collected), but then we had to push it through the sand, because no road*

existed." Visitors to Panama City Beach these days would find it nearly impossible to imagine the barren stretches of beach and the lack of utilities. Thomas built his own gathering plant [generating electricity] *with three windmill towers, a water tower and anything else that was necessary for his facility. "Don't you dare mention this," said Mrs. Pledger, "but there wasn't even a johnny out back when I came in May, 1935. I guess you know that was one of the first things I had done." A shell road was constructed as the farseeing vision of Gideon Thomas began to take shape.*

1936…Franklin Delano Roosevelt was President; America was struggling up from the great depression…and a sleepy little area on the Gulf of Mexico made the first moves toward awakening.

May 2, 1936…Ignoring problems elsewhere, gala visitors celebrated the opening of the Panama City Beach Hotel, first of its kind on the barren stretch of purest white sand. The hotel's first floor housed the dining room and bathhouse. On the second floor were twelve spacious rooms. "It seems to me," says Mrs. Pledger today, "the rooms were $4 a day." Stretching along the sparkling Gulf waters were twenty-two guest cottages. Among the guests at the grand opening was Leroy Smith of Columbus, Georgia. "Little did I realize what was going to happen," Smith says now. "Land was available for practically nothing and I was asked to invest. But what did a strip of beach mean then to a twenty one-year-old lad?" Over the years Smith came to realization as he continued his visits and watched the constant growth.

The thousand-foot Pier in front of the hotel was the focal point for visitors and fishermen. There was little else to attract anyone to the World's Most Beautiful Beach, judging by today's standards. There were no amusement parks, gift shops or garish trappings, which seem to be requisite to today's tourist. "People came here to rest and relax and to fish," says Mrs. Pledger. "There was little in the way of entertainment in those first years."

She recalled a doctor and his wife from Georgia who came the first Christmas (and returned for many years later). They arrived late in the evening, tired from their journey, and went directly to their room. "That was an unusually cold night, and when Mrs. Brickhouse awakened in the morning, she looked out the window and called excitedly to her husband about the snow that had fallen during the night," related Mrs. Pledger. "The doctor looked, started laughing, and informed her it was only the white sand drifting over the dunes." Long gone are most of the marvelous dunes. Today motels and condominiums decorate the miles of beaches. But for many years, little was there, and the only means of travel in the beach area was by foot or horseback. Few roads existed, and for many miles there

A Panama City Beach Hotel guest displays his catch at the base of the one-thousand-foot pier, late 1930s. This is not the only photo of the time period showing a gentleman fishing in his shirt and tie. *Courtesy Dennis Pledger.*

> *number swells each year as condominium and townhouses spring up, seemingly overnight. The twelve rooms and twenty-two cottages of the original Panama City Beach Hotel seem rather insignificant in number, when today there are over 5,940 motel and 2,000 condo units. But perhaps those who were here in the year 1936 saw a peaceful gracious living that will never exist again.*

From the early 1930s, young Gerden Russell, Andrew McKenzie and company had run of the Panama Theater on Harrison Avenue. Russell was the projectionist and had a movie camera as well. During the next couple of decades, Russell and the boys produced some charming and evocative newsreels of local interest to run before shows. He submitted some to *Universal News*. On August 27, 1931, the *Panama City Pilot* reported:

> *Wallace Caswell, local fisherman guide, champion wrestler with deep sea monsters…has received his first fan mail, coming all the way from Hollywood, Calif. The letter in part* [and oh wouldn't we like to get our eyes on the entire letter!], *reads: "Imagine my surprise when the other night I went to a show and was amazed to see your countenance flash before my eyes in battle with a deep sea turtle." The letter went on to say that he had best be careful, or he might break his fool neck.*

ERNIE DISCOVERS A LAND WITH A FUTURE ALONG THE GULF COAST

Before World War II, Ernie Pyle (1900–1945) took an assignment with Scripps to travel the country and write up any notable scenes he came upon. Pyle's wife was ill, and the scenery and distraction were hoped to be therapeutic. Incredibly, they made it down to St. Andrews Bay, and he describes his find in a wry voice instantly evoking the wisecracking 1930s, his sharp pen perfect for the village on the shore.

> *Say, you ought to see what I've found! It's a whole section of country that has a future. And it isn't like any other place in the United States. It gives you a funny feeling to find something like that. Makes you think you're Columbus or Cortez or one of the original Discovery Boys.*
>
> *First, let's get it located. Coming up from the west coast of Florida, you have to drive inland, behind the swamps. You never see the Gulf. You keep swinging to the northwest until you have rounded the great curve of the Gulf Coast and are up on the "mainland" of North America again. Then your road swings back south and west, and pretty soon you pop out onto the Gulf of Mexico again. There's where that stretch I'm talking about starts.*
>
> *It runs west for 26 miles to Apalachicola, on west for 65 miles to Panama City, and on west another 105 miles to Pensacola. All this coast is in Florida, but it isn't like Florida. It's far from the seething winter resorts of the lower coasts. There is practically nothing along this 200 miles of lovely coast. Just two small cities and a half a dozen cross-roads settlements. The tourists don't come this way. There are a few, of course, but they are just going through.*
>
> *Sleepy cows and half-dead razor back hogs run loose on the roadway. You have to stop dead still now and then to keep from wrapping your car around a cow. The few people, and the few towns, look neither like Florida nor the deep South. They look more like the West. Say! You see lots of goats. I saw a calf hitched up to an odd wagon.*
>
> *Panama City is the center of this 100-hile stretch. Panama City has a destiny, as sure as the sun will rise tomorrow. It is not a pretty town, but it has charm. In appearance and personality it is like a Southwest desert town. There is a great deal of white sand and not many trees. But there is a quick change at the water's edge. The town is on the banks of St. Andrews Bay, and you never saw a lovelier spot. The water is deep blue, and across the bay you see shorelines of trees, and if you look in the right*

direction you can see the opening of the tree line and beyond, the glistening water of the Gulf.

A railroad man from Chicago named George West founded Panama City 28 years ago. He opened a bank, and started a newspaper, and put in water. He is dead now. His widow still owns a good part of the city, and edits the newspaper he started. He visioned this spot as some day being a great port. He called it Panama City because it was on a direct line between Chicago and Panama, and he could see it as the teaming division point where all the Panama traffic changed from train to boat.

Five years ago Panama City had 5,000 people. [Hmm…In 1926 Panama City did a neat midnight consolidation, absorbing Millville and St. Andrews. In 1930, the town proper probably did only have 5,000 souls, but including the real 1926 city limits, the numbers would have been higher.] *Today they claim around 14,000* [numbers including Millville and St. Andrews]. *And a man who ought to know (He's not a civic booster, either) tells me that five years from now it will be 35.000.*

Unfortunately Panama City, like many little boys, is going to get ugly as it grows up. For its future depends, not on the beauty of its setting, but on industry. The biggest industry here now is the paper mill, which employs 1200 people and makes brown wrapping paper out of the Florida pine trees. The mill, two miles out of town, is a vast, smoky, odorous place, and when the wind blows right, the sickening sulphurous smell will wake you up at night. More paper mills and railroads and wharves are coming.

The road along half this 200 mile stretch of coast is new, just opened. Today, as you drive along it, you don't see a human once an hour. The sun glistens on the flat Gulf, and behind shoals the water is the color of robin's eggs. The beach, flat and white as snow, with the surf rolling endlessly on it, makes long graceful curves ahead of you, and behind. Occasionally you see schools of porpoise, leaping and playing right in the surf.

Inland it is all white sand, with scattered pine trees. There is a lonesome enchantment about it. You'd like to take a whole stretch of it, and plant some palm trees and build a cottage under them and put up a sign saying: "This is my private beach. Don't anybody come near here. I found it first." It is my guess that 10 years from now that whole 200 miles will be lined with little Palm Beaches, and tourist cottages, and life guards, and that every so often there'll be a smoking little factory city.

As a matter of fact, like so much of the South, Panama City and Panama City Beach's future depended on the U.S. government, specifically its determination to win against the Axis powers in the fight that became World War II. As Germany marched against its neighbors and Japan assaulted China, the United States quietly began to mobilize. Tyndall Air Field was established in 1941, taking all of the East Peninsula, including Crooked Island. The U.S. Coast Guard, based in the Cove, patrolled the Pass as the 1930s ended, appropriately enough, with a radio broadcast.

Lights Out on the Beach, World War II

Previously, Ernie Pyle, writing in 1936, quoted a man confidently predicting that Panama City would have a population of thirty thousand in five years, which would have been 1941. In the same article, Pyle asserts that the city's growth will stem from more industry like the paper mill, a stinky but sensible forecast. Fortunately, Bay County did not get more paper mills. When Pearl Harbor in Hawaii was bombed by the Imperial Japanese at the end of 1941, most Americans were incredulous. The news of the turmoil in Europe was in newspapers and newsreels, however, so Panama City Beach dwellers were ready to make changes if they would help protect their home from invasion.

Car headlights must be blacked out, especially along the beach. Homes must have windows covered so no light could escape and give aid to an enemy. The Japanese had just attacked a beach; the Germans were known for their U-boat aggression, so Panama City Beach became very important. As in the Civil War eighty years earlier, the bluffs at the Drummond Cut (universally referred to as the Pass) down the middle of the western tip of the lagoon's land made an excellent location to place a gun mount and a lookout, called Observation Point. Civil Defense and National Guard members patrolled the sand dunes by horse.

The dark necessity of fighting the Good War brought to Bay County the one element that has continued as its greatest blessing: people to appreciate its beauty. Certainly the empty roadways required money to pay the debts incurred to pave them, but the people brought here by Tyndall Air Base in

On the way to Panama City. A 1941 Boy Scout troop from Birmingham embarks on a camping trip. This was a hearse converted to use as a camper by Ralph Bingham Sr., who led the troop. They certainly were prepared to cook with pots and pans. *Courtesy Ralph Bingham.*

The Boy Scouts in the bay, fishing on the Binghams' boat. *Courtesy Ralph Bingham.*

1941, Wainwright Shipyard in 1942 and the naval presence in 1943 are who have made the beach so rich. Workers from Wainwright stayed at Panama City Beach Hotel, and Edgewater Gulf Apartments housed sailors here with their families. The amphibious training facility arrived in 1942. In July 2005, D. William Shephard commemorated the sixtieth anniversary of the navy base with the volume *The Early Years of the "Navy Lab"* at Panama City. He recaps the times that led to the bases' establishment here.

Memories of the "Good Old Days" at the Navy Base

The amphibious training base was established in 1942 on land the navy had previously acquired along the edge of St. Andrews Bay. Many of the men who trained at the site drove amphibious craft ashore across the beaches of the islands of the Pacific and at Normandy. As the amphibious training needs began to diminish in late 1944, the navy put the small amphibious training base into a caretaker status manned by only a skeleton crew.

In 1990, the station's historian, Mrs. Kitty Clark, interviewed a number of the station plank owners (those who were at the base at its beginning) and other early employees. They were first published in the November 2, 1990 edition of the station newspaper, *The Underseer*, and reprinted in Shephard's history, from where all of this work is reprinted.

LT(j s.) Edgar C. Blackburn, E-t (S), USNR, received orders Aus. L t s45. detaching him from duty at the Naval Mine Warfare Test station, Solomons, Md. and ordering him to proceed without delay to the U.S. Navy Mine Countermeasures Station, Panama City, Fla. He traveled by train from Washington, D.C., to Tallahassee, Fla., and reported for duty at NMCS, 11:55 a.m., Aug. 4, 1945. The following describes conditions on the edge of the bay as they were in the 1940s: Amphibious Training Base was a location used by the U.S. Navy to train U.S. fighters to land on foreign beaches. When hostilities ended, the grounds went to caretaker status. "Looking out the windows from my room I could see a beach across the bay, and across the water, a commercial shipyard where landing craft were...built."??

This narrative from Edgar Blackburn gives a good idea of what conditions were like in the 1940s.

Aerial view of Panama City Beach Resort, circa late 1930s. Looks like a lively summer day at the beach with strollers on the pier. Clockwise, the Danley house is pictured. To the east is the gatehouse, next to the iconic Panama City Beach archway. The path leads to the hotel, and to the west of the hotel is the casino, with changing rooms downstairs. The long building next to it was a shooting gallery, utilizing real .22s. *Courtesy Dennis Pledger.*

A lone lieutenant, by the name of Menendez, with about 25 men, one small motorboat and several items of rolling stock, was in charge. He told some interesting stories of problems and hardships, including one about supplying the base by boat across the bay for several weeks when the bridge was stuck open following a barge wreck. It was miles to Panama City by any other route. This sometimes unreliable drawbridge was a threat to pregnant women trying to reach the hospital from the beach.

Entry to the property was through a guard station just off U.S. 98, the beach road. A chain-link fence enclosed the property, a number of semi-wild hogs, and a majestic white long-horned steer. Domestic animals on Navy property, along the beach and on the highways were there by authority of the absence of a Florida stock law. Animal grazing had a higher priority than sunbathing, and, sometimes, of naval activities.

In spite of these sleepy conditions, there was some activity from the enemy. In 1942 a German U-boat, U67, torpedoed the tanker *Empire Mica* as it cruised off the shore of Gulf County. Thirty-three lives were lost. The propeller of the *Mica* can be seen at Captain Anderson's Marina and Restaurant at the corner of Thomas Drive.

The United States mobilized on a massive scale. Through the mettle of the fighters in all the branches of the service, combined with American dedication to producing only war necessities in factories and shipyards (by fiat or by choice), the total war was won. However, the enemy had been great, and the need for folks to fight battles, and produce ships, was great as well.

The Allied forces made compromises on with whom they'd work in Europe to defeat the Germans. In Bay County, it was supposed necessary to make sure round-the-clock shifts of workers, airmen, sailors and soldiers were fed and entertained. Local entrepreneurs built extra rooms on their homes and establishments, and businessmen and -women from other areas, such as Phenix City, opened branches here. By the cessation of hostilities in August 1945, new recreational habits had been formed, and the businesspeople we had allowed to provide pacification for the swollen population (either 30,000 or 24,000 by 1950) saw no reason to stop making good money.

The international situation was similar. We needed the Soviet machine to operate the fulcrum of the operations in Europe. After V-E Day and V-J Day in August 1945, it began to look as if the western countries of the Allied forces were going to have to reexamine their relationship with Stalin, as he initially demanded, and then took, the parts of Germany and eastern Europe he wanted.

Shephard relates that even though the war was over between the Allies and the Axis Powers of Germany, Italy and Japan, the late 1940s were not absolutely peaceful.

> *By mid-1945, against this backdrop* [of uncertainty about the motives of Soviet Russia and the future of the Western-Russian relationship], *the U.S. Navy began to prepare for the postwar era. One of the lessons learned from the war was the effectiveness of mines and torpedoes in disrupting shipping supply and amphibious operations. All of this combined to make it obvious that the Navy was going to require some sort of continuing investment in the development of methods to counter the rapidly changing mine* [and] *torpedo threat. During the war, the Navy maintained at Solomons, Maryland, a small research and test detachment that focused on mine countermeasure techniques. The site, however, suffered a number of shortcomings, not the least of which was the lack of a viable test environment.*

WELCOME BACK, NAVY!

Shephard's history continues:

> *The Navy's search for a suitable location for its mine countermeasures research efforts ended with the selection of* [the St. Andrews Bay site used by the navy during the war] *as an amphibious training base where men were trained to operate a variety of amphibious landing craft.*
>
> *The August 22, 1945 edition of the* Panama City News Herald *carried on its front page the story of the decision of the Navy to locate "… its newly technical development and research station" in Panama City.*
>
> *This story was overshadowed, however, by the day's main story as the headline proclaimed: "Tokyo Given Copy of Surrender Documents."*
>
> *A local writer by the name of Frank Pericola made the following observations:*
>
> *"Well, Uncle Sam has given the green light on the manufacture of radios and nylon hose, and also promises us more tires. We can use a new radio and the little woman no doubt will greet the nylon news with a grin, but what we need more than new tires is a new car to put 'em on.*
>
> *"Another thing Uncle Samuel said was that rent controls will be removed in areas that were war swollen and where the population has dropped considerably. Panama City may or may not come in this category.*
>
> *"'Welcome back, Navy!' The former amphibious training base is to be commissioned soon as a technical development and research station."*

WHICH NAME?

> *Since establishment in 1945, the Navy Research and Development (R&D) Laboratory located on St. Andrews Bay near Panama City, Florida, has been identified by several official Navy names. Regardless of the official designation, the R&D Laboratory has always been referred to in the local community as the "Navy Lab."*

The men who were at the navy laboratory for its first project are "plank owners." The first project was called a plank, successfully adapted at the new waterside facility for American use. Following are some memories of the early years at the navy base on the top corner of Thomas Drive, circa

John M. (Dr.) McElvey and Mrs. Elizabeth in front of the cottages they'd just built on Highway 98, 1940s. World War II workers lived here, and after the hostilities ended, they welcomed seasons of beachgoers. *Courtesy Claudia Shumaker.*

1945. We owe Mrs. Kitty Clark a huge debt of gratitude for recording these memories and Shephard many, many thanks for writing and assembling the book from which these are reprinted:

> *Jerome D. Freedman was a member of the evaluation team that made the initial inspection visit to the Panama City site to determine the suitability of the location for a mine countermeasures R&D activity. He subsequently moved from Solomons, Maryland, to Panama City. He was the Station's first Executive Officer, and served as the Station's second Commanding Officer.*
>
> *"We lived frugally on the beach* [at Edgewater Beach Apartments in the 1940s]*—no air conditioning, (and remember. we didn't even have gas stoves; we had oil-burning kitchen stoves. We learned that if you'd light it and let the flames really shoot out and then pull it off and put the coffee*

pot on, it was just right to get the coffee to boil.) We also had oil heating stoves, because there were some really cold nights.

"One of the fellows was leaving and had accumulated a bunch of cardboard boxes for packing and put them on the front porch. At that time they had the no-range law here; the cows could roam any place. In fact, they roamed on the highway and a lot of our trucks that went into Pensacola would be hitting a cow every week, so we had to put guards on the trucks to watch for cows and things. But anyhow, these boxes on the porch were apparently very attractive to these roaming cows and the next morning this fellow found the cows had eaten all the boxes. Apparently they were more tender than those palmetto leaves."

Harold A. Johnson was the first civilian (recruited by CDR Frost) to move from Solomons, Maryland, to the new Station in Panama City, Florida. Harold Johnson became the driving intellect behind the Station's technical program during the first decade of the station's existence. He had a long and distinguished career at the Station. He retired on 31 January 1969. Harold Johnson died on 11 May 2002.

"After a war, the economy tends to shrink rather than expand, so Frost [Commander T.H. Frost], *the driving force behind the mine countermeasures effort, had a tough time in Washington convincing people to come here. Panama City was isolated away from towns of any size, and commuting back and forth from Washington would be an ordeal.*

"There were no educational facilities past Bay High and no hospital except the Adams Clinic [Lisenby Hospital was built in the late 1940s]. *In fact, the biggest thing Panama City had to offer was recreation—fishing and the beach.*

"People were afraid that if they came down here, they'd be caught when places closed up and they'd have to go back to Washington to hunt jobs that might not be there. The depression of the '30s was etched in history and their memories. But Frost did a masterful selling job. He promised salaries would be good. He said we knew from history that mine warfare was here to stay, one way or the other. Frost did such a good job of selling that I packed up my wife and kids—one in the first grade and one in the fifth—and came here. I was sold. We arrived on Sunday, August 9, 1945, and started to work August 10. The shipyard [Wainwright] *closed 24 hours after we got here.*

"Frost told me to get the first significant project going…so that people in Washington would know that Panama City was serious business and the experiments underway were proof. He said, 'Give me a progress report

> *every week.' That first project was Asymmetrical Diamond. Jim Seawright arrived* [in October]. *I turned the Project over to he and Arthur Kingsley so that I could get the solenoid buildings established."*
>
> *"The CO* [Captain Goering] *was unaccustomed to the heat—to him we were in the tropics. He decided that we'd come to work early while it was cool, have a siesta period in the middle of the day, and work late when it was cool. He had us go home after work and bring our wives back for dinner and a social evening at the club."*
>
> *Plank owner James W. Blankenship remembers coming aboard in May 1946 as an auto mechanic to work in the small craft operations division. He said that T.C. Bostwick and David S. Ward were already aboard and they shared two small shacks with the military.*
>
> *"When we had an overhaul on an engine or a transmission we had to take them to a long shed where we had room to work." He said that in late 1946, a long Quonset hut was built to house the shops and "the operations division came to life."*
>
> *"The fun part was in the first few years," Blankenship said. "I worked for and with the military. We had parties, dances, fish fries, barbecues. In the winter we would fish off the docks with our wives and children.*
>
> *"We had parties in the rec hall where everyone would bring something to eat and we could buy beer at the BBQ. The jukebox never required any money, and the N.C. Meadows Band also would play for us to dance. The children were always welcome.*
>
> *"The Black Cat was the main watering hole until a mineman was refused a drink and he got two .45 automatic handguns and shot the place up. It was put off limits after that."*

Thousands of airmen, sailors, shipyard workers and soldiers—Third Army was in charge of operations at the gun mount at Observation Point—saw Panama City Beach and decided to come back after the war. Some came to visit, and some came to stay. They and their families have contributed their energy and resources to building the beach and have shaped us into the diverse community we are. Many veterans have recorded their memories of serving here, and several authors have chronicled this important time in the beach's history. Marlene Womack published *War Comes to Florida's Northern Gulf Coast*, and Gordon Steele has an interesting website devoted to the *Empire Mica*. All of these are well worth reading.

If There Were No Fools, There'd Be No Fun

If there is a place that changed as dramatically as the sky over the Gulf on a summer afternoon, it was Panama City Beach in the 1950s. In 1950, one ventured out to a remote sunny stretch of twenty-foot dunes, with a roadhouse on one end and a family hotel on the other, cows and hogs roaming freely between the two. By 1959, there were new roads, a new bridge, a restaurant that would in the future win national awards, a new look for the iconic Panama City Beach Hotel and a state park that offered access for all citizens, however imperfectly. And many, many new citizens from everywhere in the world had arrived to pad along narrow lanes bordered with sand spurs.

Quite a few of these new visitors and residents had first visited during the last war and were used to working hard and playing hard. Liquor flowed freely when the mission was accomplished, and men on furlough from the 9 to 5 planned on some R n R when they reached the beach. Businessmen who'd done well during the war providing refreshment for service personnel and war production employees were just as anxious to retain their clientele. Many visitors had new families and planned on keeping them happy and entertained, as well, which wasn't really difficult with convenient charter trips offered right down the street from the hotel room or the campsite. New conflicts and new solutions glinted on the same turquoise fish- and fun-filled waters.

In July 1959, Jesse Hassell Bryson Jr. hoists a nice catch of red snapper from an Anderson boat, a few years after the seafood company's move to Grand Lagoon. *Courtesy Marie Bryson Kelly.*

His Storehouse and Chicken Pen Were All Built with Driftwood

In 1950, Bill Snyder profiled "The Hermit of St. Andrews State Park" for *Florida Wildlife*, the official magazine of the Florida Parks Service. In fact, Teddy evidently had the park to himself in 1950. In 1953, the *Panama City News Herald* ran a squib on the front headed, "'Lack of Action' Threatens Loss of St. Andrew Park." Mrs. Elizabeth Towers, the chair of the Florida Board of Parks and Historic Memorials, sent a letter to "parks advisory councils" advising them that the lack of action, financial and otherwise, by the state was opening an opportunity for the federal government to take back lands in Florida that had been given to the state. In a delightful piece of boilerplate, longtime Bay County representative J. Ed Stokes, according to the *PCNH*, stated that "he is not thoroughly familiar with the situation but that he would 'certainly go along' with any move to provide sufficient means to 'improve and preserve our state parks.'" Radio news broadcasts and old age pensions made but brief appearances in the day of Teddy Tollofson, whose 1950 lifestyle was the epitome of the bay and beach dweller of AD 100 or of today. He lived off the abundance of the gulf, traded with his neighbors and built ingenious makeshift buildings with scavenged items.

> *Theodore Tollofson, a sturdy 76 year old Norwegian, has been living in seclusion on a remote, dune studded peninsula six miles southwest of Panama City ever since his fishing boat wrecked there in the 1929 hurricane. However, you can scarcely call him a hermit. Webster's dictionary says a hermit is a person who retires from society—and lives alone; that fails to describe Teddy because he isn't alone. You see, he's got a family with him consisting of three black cats, a one-eyed rooster, and 11 red hens—not to mention the weatherbeaten remains of his unfortunate fishing boat which he all but worships.*
>
> *No. Teddy doesn't fall into the hermit class—he's in a class all his own! For my money he's a modern-day Robinson Crusoe who has proven for 21 years that in Florida a man can keep himself supplied with fish and grits no matter what happens to him!*
>
> *Frankly, I admit that it would take a mighty rugged individual—endowed with a full tank of intestinal fortitude to follow Teddy's path since the dark howling hurricane bowled him and his boat out of the angry sea back in '29. It's more than likely that but few of us would have survived the storm itself—but Teddy did. What's more most of us would have made a one way trip to the mainland as soon as the storm subsided—but Teddy didn't. Demonstrating a shipmaster's inherent love for his craft, Teddy has stubbornly refused to leave the withering remnants of his fishing boat ever since.*
>
> *"The boat wrecked here and so we've stayed together," he told me somewhat pathetically as he reverently patted the rotting frame of his former fishing pal.*
>
> *It took two full days to get Teddy's story. You see, he's a man who weighs questions carefully before answering. His blue eyes never stop peering at you from beneath shaggy eyebrows. While talking with him you have a feeling somehow or other, that he'd rather be puttering around with a fish net or maybe feeding chickens instead of being interviewed or posed for pictures.*

To attempt writing an imitation of his fascinating dialect not only would be impossible—it would constitute pure sacrilege!

During the 21 year tenure on the wind swept sandy expanse Teddy has elected to call home, he has seen many a change occur and he's had many sad experiences that required a stout heart to forget. Yes, he's lived here long enough to watch mountainous sand dunes disappear in the path of howling winds—he's seen other dunes born in a 24 hour period. He's observed the shoreline receding inch by inch in front of the pounding waves of the Gulf of Mexico. He's watched fresh water lakes turn to salt.

Time after time, in the years gone by, sinister characters have threatened Teddy unless he'd move [from] *the government land lock, stock and barrel. But Teddy didn't bluff easily—defiantly he stayed on.*

In 1946 the Florida State Park Board acquired 758 acres of the undeveloped land from the Federal government. It's true that the abstract delivered to the Park Board accurately described the property. It traced the winding contours and placed the boundary lines: however it grossly neglected to describe Teddy—and Teddy is just as much a part of the property as the trees, the boundary lines, and the long expanse of Gulf beach!

Today the Park Department frankly admits that Teddy is equally as important to St Andrew's State Park as are the sand dunes, the shimmering lakes, and the sprawling trees. As a matter of fact, Teddy very likely is the property's most outstanding attraction.

To pay him a visit calls for considerable advance preparation. Groceries and meats must be bought to cover a two day stay. Jeeps with big tires must be procured to grind through six miles of shifting sand to reach him. There are no roads.

The thermometer was lingering in the lower 50s and the wind was hitting gusts up to 40 miles an hour one day last month when our party of eight persons started on the "Sahara safari" toward Teddy's strange home. Lewis Scoggin, state park director, headed the group. Park ranger Claude Willoughby was our guide. Since there are no roads leading to the park, we blazed our own winding trail through white sands fashioning hundreds of menacing grotesque sand dunes. [Wow! Never thought of sand dunes as menacing or grotesque. He must have been in North Africa during the war.] *Sand, shifting sand, in the high wind, lashed our faces. The scene was reminiscent of a midwinter blizzard in Ohio 40 or 50 years ago.*

Eventually we parked our camping gear and supplies in a building belonging to the park, then continued another mile or so until we arrived at Teddy's one room shack—the driftwood home he'd started building just two days after the hurricane tossed him ashore 21 years ago. Almost immediately we started interviewing Teddy—the man who, we later learned, has survived three bolts of lightning and was twice shanghaied.

First of all we were amazed at Teddy's apparent youth despite his 70 years. He was as agile as a cat. He demonstrated the stamina of a 21 year old and like I said before his memory of names and dates was astonishing. Health, I learned, has posed no problem for him during his long stay on the peninsula. However, he admits to having a cold two or three times, and once he suffered with a toothache. "What did you do for the toothache?" "Oh," said Teddy, "I yust pull him out with a pair of pincers."

Born at Trondheim, Norway, January 28, 1880, he attended school until he was 14. That's when he signed up as a seaman aboard the "Professor Johnson," a 1441-ton square rigger and took off on a 22½ month jaunt that led him to Melbourne, Shanghai, Calcutta, and Liverpool. From there on his life was just one ship after another!

The combination of too much liquor, an overnight stay in jail, and a $3.00 court fine started Teddy on his American career April 8, 1901 at Boston. He had arrived at that port several days earlier as a seaman aboard a foreign passenger ship.

"By the time I paid my fine and got out of jail, I missed my boat by 15 minutes—and so I decided to stay in America," Teddy recalled.

Then he hastened to remind us that he'd been a tee-totaler since 1907. "I quit drinking in Mobile after I figured I'd been a fool long enough," he said with a wry smile. What's more, he has never used tobacco in any form during his lifetime.

Although Teddy is a dyed-in the wool seaman, he's been a jack of all trades at various times…he once joined up with a threshing crew in the wheat fields of North Dakota in 1902. That's when he staged his first engagement with a bolt of lightning.

"A storm was coming up and I was helping a couple of children lead their pet lamb to safety."

A bolt of lightning forked its way out of a black cloud and struck. When Teddy came to, he was still grasping the end of the lead rope—the lamb was dead on the other end.

His second mix up with lightning came in 1911 while he was sailing in the Gulf aboard the "Bonita" a fishing smack.

"That time it yust knock me down on deck," he explained.

He was struck again in 1981 while walking near his present home. The bolt melted his watch that time.

"My watch stopped at 2:30 in the afternoon and when I woke up I could tell by the moon that it was after midnight," he told us. For many weeks afterward his eyes made things look like "being in a snow storm."

In 1902 he went to Seattle expecting to ship out to Alaska—but wound up in South Africa instead.

"A nice fellow gave me a drink in Seattle and when I woke up I was in Port Townsend," Teddy recalled. "Then he gave me another drink and when I came to the next time I was at sea aboard the 'Great Admiral,' a Boston tea-clipper." He remained aboard for eight months as a deck-hand at $20 monthly. When he was finally paid off, the skipper deducted one month's pay because of the trouble involved in shanghaiing him!

In 1906 he landed at Mobile on a trip from West Africa and decided to settle down at Pensacola and fish for a living in the Gulf. From then on, he usually fished alone aboard his own craft and specialized in red snappers. As a matter of fact he was snapper fishing aboard his 26 foot boat the day the 1929 hurricane broke loose and blew him ashore. During a hectic day and night, Teddy hid in a wood and frantically clung to careening trees during the storm that registered gusts up to 90 and 100 miles an hour.

"It was a bad experience." Teddy admits, "things you couldn't see were whizzing through the air and hickory nut would have dropped you like a bullet."

When the storm started subsiding he found his boat battered up beyond repair. Two days later he started building a home nearby. Timber from his boat was augmented with precious driftwood from other wreckage and the cozy 9 x 12 one room cabin was completed within two weeks.

Visiting his cabin is like making a trip to a nautical museum. The shutters swing on zinc coated skylight hinges that drifted in with ship wreckage after the '29 storm. The front door is secured by a massive padlock that likely would rate a tidy sum from an antique collector. A portion of the cornice contains the hand carved wooden name plate of the schooner, Tecumseh. Built in Gloucester, Mass in 1911 she tore up during a Gulf storm in 1921. The cabin itself is compact to say the least—containing a wood cookstove, built in table, and a bunk. Nine lanterns hang from the rafters that stand on the floor. There's a huge stack of newspapers, yellowed with age, and ancient magazines, too. However Teddy confides that he cares nothing for soap operas, mystery dramas, jazz orchestras, and the such.

"I yust listen to news broadcasts and weather reports," he told us.

Outside there's a small storehouse and a chicken pen. Even the pen gives evidence of belonging to a fisherman. It is completely screened in with a tarred seine. A short distance from the house, you'll find his "lumberyard." It contains everything from massive 10 x 10's to small sections of plywood. Every speck of it is driftwood that he has salvaged from the beach.

Then a trip down a steep slope to view the remains of Teddy's wrecked 26 footer. Pathetically, he patted the rotting timbers.

"It's all my fault it happened," he opined, "but if there weren't any fools then there'd be no fun!"

His responsibility for the wreck, he explained, came from the fact that he'd equipped the boat with a five horsepower engine. "If I'd had a 25 horse engine then this thing never would have happened," he admitted sadly, "we'd have beaten the hurricane."

When we walked away from the wreckage, Teddy glanced backward over his shoulder "One day we caught 1400 pounds of snappers—and of course, that was only one day," he whispered.

Likely by this time you're wondering how Teddy has earned a living for 21 years—how he keeps his larder supplied and still remains on the remote, sandy peninsula.

Actually, the task is an easy one for him. Every morning at the crack of dawn he is out on the beach pitching with his 15 year old homemade hickory rod and obsolete reel. During mullet season he deftly tosses his 10 foot cast net. Every morning he returns home with plenty of meat regardless of weather. What he can't eat fresh he salts down for future use. He has never used ice and as a result eggs from his hens are buried deep in the sand to keep them cool.

When the chickens need feed, or Teddy needs coffee, sugar, grits, or maybe a chunk of fresh meat, it's merely a matter of loading his skiff with fish, rowing four miles across the bay to St Andrew, selling the fish and buying the merchandise. It's a simple way of earning a living if you are endowed with Teddy's determination!

Why, we asked him, "has snapper fishing gone backward in the last few years? Do you think paper mill pollution is responsible?" Teddy didn't think so and said so. "We had paper mills in Norway when I was a boy and they didn't bother the fish," he declared, "If you ask me, it's these pesky outboard motors that are running 'em off the flats, and what don't get run off are getting killed by DDT they're spraying from the air for insects."

Maybe Teddy's got something! Frankly I don't know.

Teddy had had but a single gripe to register since he began his 21 year stay with the sand dunes and his wrecked boat. Two years ago, several youngsters entered his shack and made away with a box containing all of his important papers. Included in them were his citizenship papers. Issued at Mobile back in 1911 and his honorable discharge from the U.S. Navy at Orange, Texas on Dec 21, 1918 after the close of World War I. Federal agencies have been unable to verify the issuance of his citizenship papers, and the navy department this far has failed to locate his record as seaman. Meanwhile, although he is eligible for old age pension, he is unable to supply the required proof of age.

However, Teddy still searches vainly for a clue leading to the recovery of the lost papers He's determined too, to spend the remainder of his life with the skeleton of his wrecked fishing boat!

For my money he's a memorial to the frontiersman that has made our country the greatest in the world today, living proof that an energetic person can get his just share of fish and grits come hell or high water.

Carl Deen, the current state park director, remembers Teddy coming over to his grandparents' store at the Dothan Motel to trade. He'd row straight over from his camp to the foot of Mound Avenue, tie up and walk a block to their store, where he could turn fresh fish into coffee and other necessities.

As Bay County realized what a gem they had in the state park, the county began to use the facility for its own summer recreation programs with the schools during the summer. Students could register for the summer program and be bused out to the park and do crafts; one group built a palmetto frond shelter, and of course, there were the swimming lessons. The *PCNH* article recounts that "'Snitcher' gave the children quite a few laughs [hopefully no rabies] for she was a raccoon who stole anything she could find—especially lunches." Some of the instructors were Barbara Yost, Irma Nell Vause and Ann Pratt, all students at Florida State University. Without missing a beat, the article continues, "A similar program for Negroes was carried on at Glenwood Elementary."

Martha "Toni" Veverka was a local reporter for the *News Herald*. Additionally, she penned a "progress-sketch biography" of Walter Colquitt Sherman, "Scars of Civilization," in 1957. Here she sketches St. Andrews State Park.

Looking for something to do on a Sunday afternoon? Northwest Florida provides many and varied types of recreation within an hour's drive of Panama City. State Parks offer picnic areas fishing and swimming boating and camping facilities, and in some instances historic exhibits.

Scarcely 30 minutes from Panama City is one of Florida's most visited state parks. St Andrews State Park, 1022 acres of beach and bayfront

Many Bay County residents have fond memories of summer programs with the Bay County Recreation Department. Students met at a school in town and rode a bus to St. Andrews State Park for lessons with the lifeguards. More than one local alumnus wonders how they learned to swim in such shallow surf. 1958. *Courtesy Florida State Archives.*

property is located on Highway 392 just four miles south of Highway 98 beyond the U.S. Navy Mine Defense Laboratory.

The park opens its gates at 7 a.m. and closes at sundown. Six park rangers operate the large tract throughout the week. Two live on the grounds in addition to Park Superintendent Claude J. Willoughby, who also is supervisor for District I.

The park is one of the few in the state which has facilities for both Negro and white. Two bathing areas, each with concession stands and bath houses, accommodate [white] *and colored. A fishing pier presently is under construction at the colored beach.*

Approximately 90,000 persons have visited St. Andrews park since July 1, said a park ranger. On Sundays the average number of visitors to the recreation area totals 3000.

Swimming and boating are most popular during the spring and summer months, but fishing is a year round sport at the Park.

Summertime anglers catch hardtails and sheephead, with best fishing in April, May and June and again in late September through November according to Roy Martin, concessions operator at the park. During those months fishermen catch ling, Spanish mackerel, bonita, sheephead and mangrove snapper. Most fishing is done from a jetty several hundred feet long which separates St. Andrew Bay from the Gulf of Mexico. The northern most part of the jetties form an enclosed beach on the bay side. Here even the smallest children can play with no fear of waves or undertow. More experienced swimmers have only to cross the park to the north side for a dip in the Gulf. Concession stands provide cold foods, fishing tackle and bait.

Farther back from the bay side of the park are located a boys' dormitory and one for girls. Between them a large building provides kitchen and dining facilities. Groups visiting the park thus are permitted to stay overnight—and in many instances, several weeks. The park also provides a boat launching ramp and picnic tables. Nearby are camping facilities for trailers and tents.

The park is geared for family fun and relaxation. It was purchased by the state in 1949 and has been developed since 1955. During that time clay roads were paved, parking spaces and buildings erected.

Cost to enter the park is 25 cents per car and fees are used from park maintenance, the ranger said.

The twenty-first-century reader may have started after reading the Veverka article in the 1958 Panama City paper where she proudly notes that the park had "facilities for both Negro and white." In fact, that was the result of moral courage in the face of political suicide from a twenty-four-year-old white kid from the sticks named Jack Mashburn. Somehow he had the foresight to insist that when the Florida legislature, to which body he had somehow just gotten himself elected, wrote the bill to better fund the park before it reverted back to the U.S. government, that they'd better make sure it included facilities for "Negroes."

The section of the state park that was designated "colored" was owned and run as a beach concession by Hubert Brown back in the late teens or early 1920s. At some point during that time, it was the only Washington/Bay County Gulf beach that black people were "allowed" to visit for recreation.

Local historian Robert Cain remembered, "We knew where the limit was." He recalled enjoying the visits; his parents would fish, and he "love[d] to see the Gulf, and loved to get in the sand, and the waves, and play in the plants" on the dunes. He visited before the early 1950s when the "new" bridge was built and the state park "improved." When he and his family took a beach trip from their neighborhood on the "Hill" near St. Andrews, they went down what is now Thomas Drive, avoiding horses and other animals

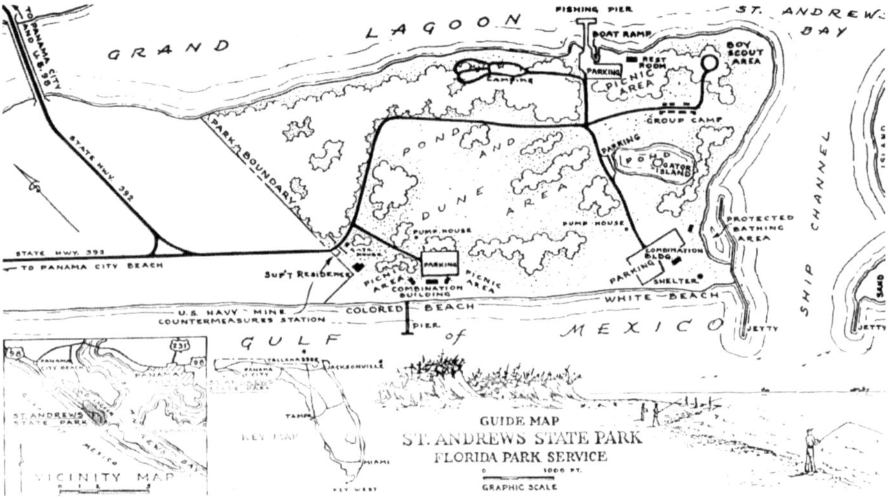

This 1962 map of St. Andrews State Park depicts a peaceful scene of surf fishing. It also delineates an area around the Gulf pier as the "colored" area. As shocking as a segregated beach may be to modern-day readers, the idea of allowing black people on the beach at all was controversial in the 1950s in other parts of Florida. In 2010, Michelle Obama held a news conference on the beach slightly west of this location, in her capacity as First Lady of the United States of America, during the BP oil disaster response. *Courtesy Local History Room, Bay County Public Library.*

on the way. He had no fear of them; they had always been loose, one might say "free" to walk anywhere they chose. When the family made it to the lagoon, they'd have to park the car. The old wooden bridge was too rickety to dare take a car over. Of course, if you had a job at one of the places on the beach, you could catch the Greyhound, as Robert's mother did. She worked at Long Beach and had worked at Panama City Beach Resort as well.

Years later, in the 1950s, a Rosenwald High School basketball star had similar experiences. He and his friends visited the "colored" beach at the state park. Since the sand was all the uniform white God had made it, someone had helpfully run a rope out 150 yards into the Gulf so that the black beachgoers would "know better" than to go to the east of that demarcation. The Rosenwald student, who did not want his name used, said, "We just went to Port St. Joe." But he was able to work at Captain Anderson's first restaurant out on the edge of the lagoon. He started, in high school, as a dishwasher making six dollars a day and later graduated to busboy, which he liked, since busboys were able to make tips as well as wages. He went away to college and ended up in Chicago, where he's had a rewarding career combining education with his love of basketball.

As retrogressive as these stories sound, St. Andrews State Park was quite liberal. By 1958, Panama City's unofficial gulf rival, St. Petersburg, Florida, had closed Spa Beach to "prevent mixing of whites and Negros." A black doctor there, Fred Alsup, participated in a four-year suit, *Alsup v. St. Petersburg*, which "broke down enforced segregation at the Spa facility" on the Gulf. So in spite of the shortsightedness of some in Panama City Beach, the area inadvertently came out looking near progressive in comparison to some other Deep South beaches in the 1950s.

In 2010, in response to the BP Deepwater Horizon oil explosion disaster, Michelle Obama, wife of Barack Obama, the president of the United States, stood a few hundred yards from the area of old Brown's Beach (which some African American residents remember calling "Black Beach") as reassurance that the administration was aware of the events in the Gulf. In her remarks, she laughed, "I've got sand in my shoes. I guess that means I have to come back." A few weeks later, the Obama family (except daughter Malia, who was away at camp) were seen by the world dining at Bay Point and frolicking with the dolphins on Alligator Point.

Jack Mashburn was evidently one of the few who could see that coming. The Bay County native has filled a lot of his years here doing the most good for the most people, as his father advised him.

Virginia Dixon follows that dictum as well. She has spent years teaching English and language skills to Bay County students, working with the Historical Society of Bay County and writing. She published *Where's Willie*, a children's selection that spotlights conservation of the area's natural resources. She leads writing workshops and has a dream of making quality books available to all children at no cost. She wrote the following for *Panama City Living* in 2010:

> *Although he only served one term, Jack Mashburn was the moving force that created many of the resources we now enjoy. On May 2, 1952, he was elected to represent Bay County in the Florida Legislature. He had announced his candidacy when he was only twenty-two years old and working as a lab technician at Arizona Chemical with Grady Courtney, who was the representative at the time. When his co-worker told Jack that he was not running for re-election, Jack said, "Well, I'm running for your seat." He laughs as he recalls, "Everybody but me took it as a joke, but I beat two prominent people."*
>
> *Jack will tell you, "My father told me to do the greatest good for the largest number of people over the longest period of time, and every decision*

I made was based on that." A product of a long line of pioneers, Jack Mashburn is the epitome of the character that built this community: he did the right thing even when he knew it would cost him the next election. His father had taught him to be tough and make the best use of what resources he had.

Jack's mother, Lillie Lee Seay, first married George Land, and after having two children with him became a widow when he died of pneumonia. Jack's father, Mansel DeShong Mashburn, had five children by his first wife who died. Lillie and Mansil were married in 1927, and on April 21, 1928, Jack was born. "There were nine of us all together, and Dad used to say 'mine, yours, and ours,' but it seemed like all one bunch to me."

Jack still lives in the old home place with his half-sister, Velma Pauline Land, whom he has cared for since her stroke. She cared for him after he was born with what some might call a birth defect. His right hand is a nub, but he calls it a "birth asset."

Jack recalls that when he was three his father built him a small wooden box and filled it with sand. Manse, as he was called, said, "Start hitting in there, Jack. You'll have that nub for the rest of your life. Start using it," and so Jack did. When he was required to pick peas, Jack asked his dad how he expected him to pick so many with one hand. Manse replied, "Pick twice as fast with the hand you got." Jack out-picked every brother and sister. Today, he can type 50 words per minute.

Jack often has visitors to his home where he grows blueberries and grapes and gathers honey from bees. Kind and generous, Jack shares his bounty. Recently, a five-year-old girl who was visiting with her parents asked him if she could see his "little hand," he replied, "You may," and squatted down to talk to her at eye level. "This is how God made me. Even when I was a little baby, it was like this. You see, God knew I had so much ability, I didn't really need these fingers." She asked, "Can I touch?" He was "tickled to death" and smiled as she put out a little finger and felt his nub. She said, "It sure is strange, but I love you." Tears welled up in Jack's eye as he told her he loved her, too.

That little girl probably doesn't know that when she goes to St. Andrews State Park with her family, she can thank Jack Mashburn for the opportunity. St. Andrews State Park is now the most visited state park in Florida, but it almost failed to become a state park at all. The property had been designated a state park in 1946; the federal government released the property provided Bay County and the State of Florida built a place that was actively used as a park; however by 1953, nothing had been done to improve access to the land so that it could accommodate visitors. Mashburn explains, "The General Accounting Office in Washington sent the State word to the effect if it was not going to be used as a State Park, they were going to take back the land. I knew we could not let that happen, so I drafted legislation that nailed it down."

Jack says, "That legislation included language that created space inside the park for Blacks. There were some folks who were opposed to the bill, but my father had taught me to always do the right thing. Not the popular thing, but the right thing. And this was quite unpopular. In fact, a whole busload came to Tallahassee, I think with tar and feathers, but not being desirous of being tarred nor feathered, I wouldn't meet them at their motel. I told them, 'I will set aside a meeting room at the Capitol because if I am going to get hung, I want it done publicly with pictures.'"

True to his word, the twenty-four year old set up a meeting room. He recalls: "They asked me, 'Why are you doing this to us?' I told them, 'I am not doing this to you. I am doing this for you. Are you familiar with the US Supreme Court? Have any of you heard the issue of Brown v. Topeka Kansas School Board*?' They said, 'No,' so I told them, 'There is a man who has sued the Board of Education for not allowing his eight-year-old daughter to attend the brand new school built next to his house. She has to be bused all the way across town. He is going to win that suit, and that is going to integrate our park.'" Jack knew that integration was coming and that the community was not prepared for it. "All our tourists back then were pea pickers, peanut pickers, and factory workers, and this is not derogatory because I am in the classification myself. They were not ready for integration. I said, 'One axe-handled or hoe-handled fight where our tourists' children are maimed and they will stay away from here, so I am doing this for you not to you. I don't know any other way to tell you, but the bill will remain as it was written.' So next they sent three businessmen, they are all dead now, but I won't mention their names... and they wanted me to have breakfast with them. After we had finished breakfast, one of them told me, 'We understand you insist on putting in a park for Negroes.' I told them, 'You understand correctly.' They said, 'Well, we came prepared to talk you out of that.' I said, 'I didn't hear that, but the second time will constitute an attempt to bribe an elected official.' One of them said, 'I'm not believing what I am hearing.' I said, 'Did I not speak clear enough? I'll be glad to repeat it. The bill stays and I'll not change it.' One of the people, who owned property* [near the park] *said, '... They'll be running up and down the beach.' I bit my tongue real* *hard and I said, 'I will make you a solemn promise. If you will call me when the first one leaves a black footprint, I'll come clean it up.' They said, 'We'll take care of you the next election.' And I told them, 'That's the American way.'" Holding a copy of the bill that he helped pass, he says, "It was the first park on the Gulf of Mexico from Brownsville, Texas, to Key West, Florida, to allow a black person to put a foot on the sand or in the water without the chance of being arrested."*

Jack is also proud of his legislation that created the first city at Panama City Beach. The Florida Constitution gives each city or municipality the right to regulate the sale of intoxicating beverages. At the time, Bay County and the City of Panama City could set their own rules regarding the hours of operation for selling spirits. Jack recalls, "At one time, there were 23 supper clubs, where you could go and see a play while you ate… but at twelve o'clock at night, you couldn't have a bottle or a glass of wine at your table. They had to be lifted and moved away; it didn't matter if the glasses were full or empty. And it was driving business away from the beach. They were leaving here like Moses leading the Israelites out of the desert. They were going to Orange Beach, Pensacola, and other places, so I told myself, if I could do nothing else, at least, I would give them some self-autonomy."

The business community wanted a city from bridge to bridge from Phillips Inlet to Hathaway Bridge, but Jack said, "You can't do that because anyone living in the incorporated area can petition the circuit court in the area in which you live to furnish three things: adequate water, adequate sewage, and adequate police." He explains, "In 1953, there was no way they could afford to run a water line from bridge to bridge; there would have to be a tax so high it would run away business. So I suggested a compromise. Do one city from 'The Y' to Hathaway Bridge and one city from 'The Y' to Phillips Inlet. They said 'No, we want it all or we want nothing.' I told them, 'I don't want to make all of you mad, but you ain't gettin' nothing and you ain't gettin' it all.' So I created six separate midget municipalities. It incorporated the areas where the supper clubs were so they could set their hours of sales of beverages legally. It would also give those operating the city a chance to learn how to operate a city. You can't just start off with a 22 mile long city." Jack was right. As the years passed, the community grew and created more cities until they combined the cities into the City of Panama City Beach.

Every person who has ever been to Tommy Oliver Stadium can thank Jack for that, too.

Jack graduated from Bay High School in 1936. Years later his coach, Tommy Oliver, enlisted to serve in World War II and was killed in action. In 1954, while Jack was in office, the school board wanted to build a stadium for the high school but didn't have the money to do so. Jack is especially proud of his part in helping secure the funding, but he says, "I don't want to take all the credit though. We had two representatives: J. Ed Stokes and I came up with an idea of setting aside $10,000 from the race-track funds for twenty years. They needed $200,000 to build a stadium. Back then, as is now, a certain portion from every racetrack, pari-mutuel pools, and jai alai frontons funds were put in a lump sum and each of the 67 counties got so much. By this bill, for twenty years we set aside that, and they went out and bonded that and got the $200,000 to build it. The class of '56 was the first class to get to use it." No property taxes were used to build the stadium, just the revenues from recreational betting in Florida.

During Jack's two-year term, he helped create the legislation that erected new bridges to the ever growing beaches and Tyndal Air Force Base. He also co-authored the bill that created a medical and nursing school at the University of Florida, now known as Shands Hospital. After serving as a representative he returned to his hometown and his job. He later became the union representative and in 1979 he retired. Since then he has remained busy in his community, serving on many boards. He is presently the Chairman of the Bay Soil and Water Conservation District and has been for 31 years. The job pays nothing.

Today visitors to Camp Helen State Park can thank Jack for that, too. Jack personally got a thousand signatures and was part of a group that went to Tallahassee to lobby for the park. They presented the ten thousand signatures that moved it up to number 27 on the acquisitions list, but then they learned that the State wouldn't consider it unless it was in the "top ten." After presenting underwater photography of the coral reefs off Camp Helen, the site was moved up to number six, but the State had no money. Jack knew what to do. "It so happens that at that time, a friend of mine, George Wilson, was the head of the Nature Conservancy in Florida, so I said, 'Let's go talk to George.' They bought that land and held it until the State got its money and didn't charge them a dime in interest. As far as I know, we are the only county in the State of Florida that has a state park on either end of our beach. Aren't we lucky, Bay? The parks are the future. It is like building a road, a bridge, or an airport: they are built for the future, not for the present."

> *In a book that he co-authored with Marlene Womack,* The Rich Heritage of Panama City Beach and Communities of Bay County, *Jack explains his belief: "We all have a vested interest in remembering the past, celebrating the present, and inspiring the future. The past asks only to be remembered, the present seeks only to be enjoyed; the future, however, requires dedicated planning with an inspired vision." Always looking to the future, Jack says, "I was thinking of telling Jimmy Patronis that what we need is a rubber-tired people mover at Camp Helen to get people from the visitor's center out to the beach. It is 1,600 feet to the beach, and it is a hard walk for me now, but one day I expect to get old one day and might need it." There is little doubt that the future includes a "people mover" to ferry people to the beach at Camp Helen.*

The *Panama City News Herald* amplifies Mr. Mashburn's recollections. In an article dated March 5, 1953, it was reported that J.E. Churchwell, A.W. Pledger and M.C. Buckley "voted against incorporating the entire [beach from Phillips Inlet to the Hathaway Bridge] area at a meeting held… at Laguna Beach." Speaking for the group, Buckley said, "We attended a meeting a year ago at the 98 Club that was called to get the beaches incorporated. That was after the [Bay] County Commission had ruled there would be no whiskey sales on Sunday. I made the statement at that meeting that I am not against any club operators, but I don't feel it's fair to the public to incorporate and put high taxes on the people just so whiskey can be sold on Sunday." The article continues, "Buckley explained that incorporation would remove the beaches from the whiskey sale jurisdiction of the county commission." Churchwell added some ideas of his own: "If we have five corporations, then we have five mayors. Each mayor will have new ideas, different ideas, and the promotions they work on will encourage new visitors. But if we have one…sparsely populated 16 mile area…it would be impossible to provide proper taxation and proper benefits for everybody."[§] Churchwell made the same forecast as Jack Mashburn, and indeed, in 2011, between the bridges are still many empty fields, many empty condos and entire ghost divisions, little white round tombstones sticking out of the sand.

§. Like the giant metal bumper tags? "Don't you tell anyone this," began a certain person who grew up with his family on Panama City Beach in the 1940s and '50s. "We used to sneak up on cars that had that big metal tag; it was attached with wires, big letters, 'Long Beach.' Well, we'd go take them off cars and throw them away. We thought we were helping. Our dad did NOT think like that." The boy, now far from the arm of his own father or J.E. Churchwell, looks grave and shakes his head.

"On your beach Helen Colee, 1955," in front of the Panama City Beach cottages. *Courtesy Dennis Pledger.*

Pledger agreed. "The problems of all the beaches are not the same. Each one has problems peculiar to its own area like life guards and lifesaving equipment." Pledger also pointed out: "In 1935 we established the name Panama City Beach for that one beach on the east end. Now it's all known as Panama City Beach. When we pioneered out there it was nothing, just sand dunes. I think it's unfair to establish one municipality using the name Panama City Beach."

A few days later, on March 11, the *PCNH* printed a letter it had received from—well, you'd better read it yourself:

> *A group of 10 beach beverage dealers denied yesterday afternoon the existence on the beaches of a "Retail Liquor Dealers Association." In addition, they "wholeheartedly agree to the abolishment of liquor sales on Sunday."*
>
> *Some opponents to the proposed incorporation of the beaches have objected to on grounds that the move was being pushed by membership of a "Retail Liquor Dealer's Association" in order to open the area for Sunday sales of alcoholic beverages.*
>
> *The dealers said in the letter, "We the undersigned beverage dealers of the beaches outside of Panama City, and legal taxpayers...are operating*

Dr. J.R. McElvey and his grandson Joseph display a grand sailfish they caught in the Gulf not far from the McElvey Cottages, background. Late 1950s. *Courtesy Claudia Shumaker.*

businesses voted on by the people of Bay County and are and have been conducting business in a clean and respectable manner. It takes all kinds [misprinted in the paper as "kids"] *of operations to build a community…and the taxes we pay…go a long way toward making Florida's highways and schools among the best of the country.*

"We are law abiding citizens… We feel that we are justly due a day of rest ourselves. We do feel, however, that our law enforcement officers should work hard and diligently to abolish sales of illegal whiskey in its entirety from Bay County and we believe they are earnestly trying to do this.

"We would like to most emphatically deny…the existence on the beaches of a Retail Liquor Dealer's Association. Many times in the past few weeks statements have been made to [that] *effect…with Mr. J.R. (Dick) Arnold as its president. In all fairness, these statements should have been denied long ago. Mr. Arnold is not in the liquor business, nor has he been for a good many years.*

"We as individual dealers, are desirous of bringing the true facts to light. Last summer the sale of liquor on Sunday was abolished by the County

Holiday Lodge was a ranch-style luxury resort at the foot of the Hathaway Bridge. It featured bay swimming, boating and quick access to the Gulf. Holiday Lodge offered fine dining, swimming (shown) and a golf course on the grounds. The "resort council," the precursor to the Tourist Development Council, met there. A local journalist, Larche Hardy, recalled, "It was…also once the Sheriff's [Lavelle Pitts] command post for one of the many hurricanes. I recall water almost lapping at the front door during the height of one of the [squalls going through]." *Courtesy Florida State Archives.*

> *Commissioners on the beaches, but sales of mixed drinks were allowed in the adjacent City of Panama City in places where food was served. We felt we were being discriminated against…and called a meeting of the beverage dealers of the beaches. Mr. Arnold was called about thirty minutes in advance of that meeting. He made it clear he was not presiding…but would do all he could to get us equal rights with Panama City. He stated that his name could be used in any way that would benefit us. Since…Mr. Arnold's cooperative attitude has been used as a weapon against him. Since he has not come forward with denials himself, we think it's high time that we did. Mr. Arnold is one hundred per cent for the growth and development of the beaches and the subsequent growth of Panama City itself…*
>
> *"We hope that the foregoing will straighten out false impressions left with your readers in this matter."*

The *PCNH* closed the letter: "The letter was signed by C.M. Fernandez, Little Birmingham; H.M. Burnette, The Frolic Restaurant and Bar; J.H.

A two-story beach cottage on Panama City Beach. Alice Jenkins summered here in the 1950s. She and her husband, Eugene Goins, got one of the first lots in Holiday on the Beach and built a two-story there, now used by their grandchildren. *Courtesy Ginger Dempsey.*

Needham's store, early 1950s, after the J.R. Needhams migrated to the warm shores of the Gulf. Son Tommy stayed and finished studies at his West Virginia college, where he developed his interest in photography. He followed his parents down and joined them on Panama City Beach, framing the beauty of the east end with his lens for the next forty years. *Courtesy Local History Room, Bay County Public Library, Needham family.*

Freiley, Beach Liquor and Package Store; J.D. Brandt, Georgia-Alabama Package Store; Charles A. Hall, Playhouse; J.T. Meadows, Plaza Chef; M.L. Cobb. 98 Club; Lea Ellen Cittandini, H.H. Lambert, Old Dutch Inn; and W.H. Beckham, The Y Bar."

Mr. Mashburn's sound reasoning worked out satisfactorily for Angus Wilson Pledger, a Jackson County native who had given up his Jacksonville home in 1935 to live on the empty beach. His father-in-law (guess which county he was from?), Gideon Thomas, had asked Pledger to come back with his daughter, Claudia Octavius Thomas Pledger, to help run the resort he'd envisioned in the sand. Thomas had previously dreamed up the edenic idea of a two-thousand-acre "Sweetwater Ranch" up near North Bay. By 1930, he had set myriad species of lithesome deer to roam over a countryside laced with hardwoods and small streams. Unfortunately, Mr. Thomas had not foreseen that the deer would leap like gazelles over the iron and cypress enclosures. The January 8 issue of the *Panama City Pilot* recounted that Mr. Thomas had dammed a pond and filled it with fish. "All Mr. Thomas has to do is go…to the pond and whistle, and up come the fish to be fed. This [for the *Pilot*] is a novel instance, for seldom if ever before have the majority of us heard of pet fish."

In spite of this rare miscalculation on their father's part, the young marrieds joined Claudia's dad and mother, Lavenia (Dolly), and worked. The feminine touch—the city touch—was just what the place needed. Gideon Thomas thought, planned, worked and built. Even if no plant in the South would ever grow here, his dreams had found fertile ground. There was good, sweet water—the tourists from camps and other hotels and cottages would come and buy or beg some of the tank water from the Panama City Hotel. The hotel had its own windmills generating electricity. They even sold it back to Gulf Power in the early days. In 1940, the Pledgers adopted two little boys, Angus Dennis and Gerald Thomas. They frolicked and worked on the beach alongside their whole family and extended family of workers and guests. When the time came to attend school, their dad drove them every day to Cove School and then drove them back out to the bright sunny expanse of cerulean that was their backyard. A dusty little scratch of grass bordering a dustier little sand path was their front yard; they had the "guard house" next to the PANAMA CITY BEACH archway for themselves and their parents.

Like G.M. West in Old Town twenty-five years before, eighteen- and twenty-hour days may have exacted a price from Gideon Thomas. He died still a young man. His wife and children continued on. Claudia had

March 31, 1953. The grand opening of Thomas Drive is attended by J. Ed Stokes, Mrs. J.M. (Elizabeth) McElvey, Bay County commissioner B.V. Buchannan, Ruth McElvey (Harrington) and Linda Hill, Gideon and Lavenia (Dolly) Thomas's granddaughter. *Courtesy Claudia Shumaker.*

taken right to the business, and as more people began to come down and set up shop, it became that much nicer. They became fast friends with the McElveys, who ran a drugstore and a couple of hotels down the street. The ladies worked to get Gulf Beach Baptist (the Pledgers) and Gulf Beach Presbyterian (the McElveys) established.

In 1953, all sorts of stuff transpired in Tallahassee. Through the auspices of Mr. Thomas, land had been donated for road improvement on the beach. On March 31, 1953, the brand-new Thomas Drive was dedicated and the ribbon cut. Mrs. McElvey was the official hostess and arranged the celebration. Mrs. Dolly read a note of thanks with her children and grandchildren around her. The bigwigs came out; even the commander of the navy mines countermeasures station was on hand, no doubt relieved to have a passable roadway in front of his installation.

As a result of the incorporation fracas, Panama City Beach Resort became Panama City Beach City, and Claudia Thomas Pledger became

McELVEY'S COURT

"BY THE SEA"

WEST HIGHWAY 98 ADams 4-131

Above: A 1954 United States Geological Survey Map, detail east end of Panama City Beach, St. Andrews Bay. *Courtesy Ralph Bingham.*

Right: McElvey's Court, Panama City Beach. In addition to the drugstore and the cottages, the McElveys operated a hotel on the Gulf. *Courtesy Local History Room, Bay County Public Library.*

John Daniel saw plenty of promise in the bright white sand as well and set his son up in business. John Daniel Jr. operated the Sand Box on Thomas Drive in the summers after the 1952 opening of the new bridge over Grand Lagoon. *Courtesy Frances McDonnell.*

its first mayor. Their son Dennis cared not about who sold what; he said, in fact, that even if his beliefs had not included a proscription against alcohol, he didn't want to mess with selling it. He'd seen what it did to people and, furthermore, would have been against slots had he had any say in it, but since they came back in when he was an infant, he did not.

Nancy Bryant remembered just the kind of trouble that machine in the big central hallway could get a girl. When Birmingham's Republic Steel would go down for maintenance in the summer, her older brother would take her and her sisters and cousins—whoever got in the car—down for a couple of weeks on the beach. They stayed wherever had a vacancy and had fun in the sun. Her brother had put the slots off limits in no uncertain terms. Nancy, about fourteen, headed for the Panama City Beach Hotel, where they often bought ice and water, and hit the machine. Jackpot! Dimes, dimes and more dimes, everywhere! All over the floor! She won! What in the world would she do with them? And what was her brother going to do when he found out? She doesn't remember how she got there, but when she got to the room, she stuffed the dimes in the back of her pillow, and her brother never knew. She had pin money the rest of the trip but felt bad the whole time.

Later, Dennis Pledger (now grown with a beautiful wife—"the most consistent Christian I've ever known," he says plainly) proposed on the same pier he and his brother ("you don't need to put this in your book") jumped off as kids when no one was looking, in front of his "house." When he came back to the beach after playing farm ball with the Detroit Tigers and a career as a Florida state patrol officer, he opened his own resort—a camping resort down the street, Pledger's Campers' Inn.

In fact, that's how this editor was introduced to Mr. Pledger, or Pastor Pledger, as he was called by a couple of generations of members at Gulf Beach Baptist Church. At the new beach library, during a conversation with its director, Frank, the words Panama City Beach were mentioned. A man presumably next in line for the desk jumped in and said, "I know just who you need to talk to! Dennis Pledger! Let me tell you a story—He was running that campground and two spring breakers with long hair came up and said, 'Where can we buy some beer?' And nice as you please, he said, 'You're welcome here, but if that's what you want to do, you'll be happier somewhere else,' and they moved on." The angel in the white T-shirt offered Mr. Pledger's phone number and said, "You can tell him I told you to call." If you're able to serve as pastor and a Bay County deputy, and run a campground simultaneously, then evidently you've earned the right to do things the way you like.

A Full-Fledged Member of the "Fun" Section

If the calendar said "1960"—so odd, so futuristic compared to the way fives look on the page—then the east end of the beach certainly found itself at a new juncture. In January 1960, there was a roadway around the peninsula. There was a modern state park visited by folks from, well, at least all over the Southeast, many of whom would come back for decades, first with spouses and then children, relaxing alone again, and then with an RV full of grandchildren. "[Coming to the park] becomes a way of life," said St. Andrews State Park director Carl Deen. There were brand-new modern rooms with a new modern look, rainbow sherbet–painted doors at Panama City Beach Motel, as well as a string of the cutest little space pod travel trailers lining the shore to the west. There were new summer cottages set among the dunes. These squat rectangles made of concrete blocks may not have won the aesthetic prizes the year they were built, but their sandy terrazzo floors are etched in the memory of many a beachgoer. And unlike many beach structures, these live on outside of the mind, one on Elizabeth, some on Sunset, several on the lagoon. They are fireproof and storm resistant, like the decade's new Grand Lagoon bridge.

The technicians at the navy lab continued their ultra-modern business of keeping us safe from Communist threats, working long hours and playing long hours. A photo shows a group relaxing together after bowling night at a home in Woodlawn, the new subdivision across Highway 98 from the navy

The New Panama City Beach Resort. In 1957, with the Pledger boys in school, the decision was made to sell the hotel on a lease option to Ed Faile. In 1958, the beautiful old pine structure burned. Said Dennis, "I cried as I left" the hotel grounds after viewing the site. The Pledgers took back the property and began again. "I wanted to build a three-floor structure," but the family went with the strip style popular at the time. They did set out trailers on the west side, a new sort of beach cottage. *Courtesy Dennis Pledger.*

Jesse Bryson in the popular plastic boat, Alligator Point, circa 1969. *Courtesy Marie Bryson Kelly.*

base. Here, many of the young scientists and their bright, pretty young wives began families and hosted parties (and *lots* of relatives during the summer months). It was good enough for Dempsey Barron and his family, and he spent much of his year as a new representative in the capital, Tallahassee.

Even Bay County government took notice. Just a few years before, Jack Mashburn, farsighted as he was, had cautioned the Andersons about going out to the lagoon in the middle of nowhere. Who'd ever even find them besides black people, hit men and Bay High teens? But the old customers did follow them after they got moved off their downtown property. Even more visitors flocked to the fishing charters, enough that the Andersons had to build a new glass-walled restaurant, like something in California, like nothing else here.

Roy Martin, fishing kid, the Needham boy's buddy—not only did he (and his wife!) reel in some magnificent fish, but he also wrote about it. He and a Woodlawn resident, Ray Patrick, went to fish fests with other *Outdoors* writers and really put Panama City Beach, the Gulf Lagoon Beach, what have you, on the map. So now the chamber of commerce took notice. Panama City Beach

Marie Bryson Kelly: "Believe it or not, Mom always actually cleaned and cooked [fried] all these little fish we always caught!" Marie Bryson, Philip Bryson and Jesse Hassell Bryson Jr., Alligator Point, 1969. *Courtesy Marie Bryson Kelly.*

started being called inside when company came, introduced to the folks. Of course, when the grown-ups had business to discuss, Panama City Beach was encouraged to go back out and play, which it was quite happy to do. For now.

The streets still rolled up after Labor Day. There was now an elementary school, Beach, to the west, but all the other children had to ride to Bay High, which didn't bother them too much. How many students riding the school bus get to watch dolphins dive? The kids certainly were the envy of most of the students in Georgia and Alabama, who were in Panama City en masse for SAE weeks in the spring after coming here as babies with their parents or sometimes grandparents. There was a new road, but that was it. It was still just as handy to ride a horse over the towering sand dunes as it was to

The McElvey granddaughters, Charla, Claudia and Carol Collins, spending the summer on the Gulf, early 1960s. *Courtesy Claudia Shumaker.*

try to drive anywhere. If teenage boys came out from town, as one of them, Carl Bennett, remembers, "a pickup truck, 2x6s and a shovel were standard equipment" because more than likely you'd get stuck in the sand.

In the 1930s, Ernie Pyle predicted additional heavy industry would ensure Panama City's growth. World War II intervened, and the cold war thoughtfully maintained some of Bay County's growth, since Tyndall Air Force Base and the navy lab were actively protecting the United States. against the Red Menace. As leaders here began to realize how much money those tourists were leaving on "the beach," so, too, were the townsfolk of Destin and Orange Beach. It was decided that the visitor should be alerted to the special delights of Bay County's sugar sand shores. Beginning around 1960, a printing firm was enlisted to highlight what was now being called the "Miracle Strip." The established resorts were heavy sponsors. However, smaller blocks of motels begun by couples looking forward to a working retirement spent on the Gulf of Mexico became known as the mom and pops. They knew the value of advertising as well and are represented attractively in the pages of the tourist tabs and, even more so, in the warm memories of folks who visited the same motels year after year. Let the scribe of the *Panama City Visitor* transport the reader along the blinding white beach and foot-searing pavement of Thomas Drive. Watch out for the sand spurs!

SCENIC THOMAS DRIVE

Scenic Thomas Drive, offering the luxury accommodations and recreational activities for which the beaches are widely noted, has only developed into a full-fledged member of the "fun" section of Panama City in the past few years.

Named in memory of beach pioneer Gideon M. Thomas, who settled the area before electricity was available, Thomas Drive turns left off U.S. 98 at Long Beach. Either route passes the popular Signal Hill Country Club with its lush golf greens.

Nearby are wild sand dunes where much beach photography is shot; white rolling sand touching emerald green waters, waving grasses and sea oats combine to create a blend that is sheer joy to the photographer.

Further east are residential areas, where houses are located with back doors opening on the Gulf of Mexico; swimming is only a few steps away. Here too are motel and apartment complexes and restaurants.

The most complete and convenient facilities are offered by such accommodations as the Pana Roc Motel, Fred Johnson Motel, Sun-N-

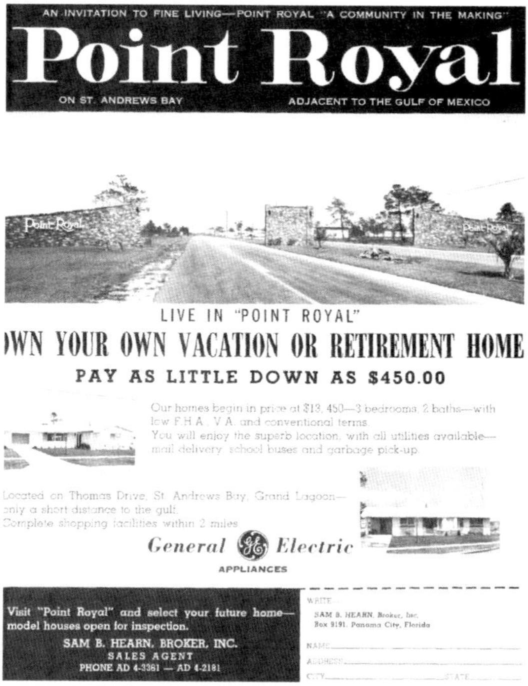

This 1963 advertisement promises you can "own your own retirement or vacation home" and "Live in Point Royal." Today, most folks racing past on Magnolia Beach Road may not realize the ultra-convenient neighborhood behind Winn-Dixie has a name, but Angela Sullivan remembers moving in as a very young girl at the time this ad was running. Since her parents were one of the first buyers, their home was custom built, featuring a garage and extra space. She grew up there and married, and she and her husband are raising their family in the same home. *Courtesy Local History Room, Bay County Public Library*.

Advertisement for Signal Hill Country Club, noting "SAND DUNES ON THE GULF," circa 1967. The high hill still on the course is reputed to have been used to signal vessels on the Gulf coming in to St. Andrews Bay. *Courtesy Local History Room, Bay County Public.*

George Baker rides Champ and Charlene Hale steers St. Cloud down one of the large dunes that covered the area near the intersection of Joan Avenue and Thomas Drive. This 1967 photograph shows the beach now covered by Club La Vela's swimming pool. *Courtesy George Baker.*

Swim Motel, Gulf Crest Motel, Merri-Mac Motel, Ebb Tide Motel, Biltmore Beach Motel, Oxford Motel and Beach Colony Motel. Just off Thomas Drive are the Magnolia Beach Campgrounds and Alligator Point Campgrounds.

As the drive swings north, a paved road travels east to St. Andrews State Park; boasting a wildlife refuge, the park has some of the area's best fishing at the "Jetties." Just past the park, Thomas Drive goes past the Grand Lagoon Bridge, where many fine boating facilities are available. Accommodations include launch ramps, wet and dry storage and charter and party fishing boats.

On the lagoon you will find Fishland USA (Unusual Sea Animals), the area's only seaquarium. Operated by fisherman Roy Martin, this interesting attraction features two sea lions, a 2235-pound frozen whale, a 400-pound sea turtle and various live and mounted fish specimens.

One of the long-lamented mom and pops, the Beach Colony, highlighted in this 1969 ad, was not the victim of greed but of the Earth's rotation and thermal distribution system—namely, a hurricane. A wire photo shows the once delightfully acid-hued patios pitifully caved in by the winds. Town houses stand there now, but the same mom and pops that shared the street with the Beach Colony brim full of multigenerational families in the summer and fall and the first generation in the winter. *Courtesy Local History Room, Bay County Public Library.*

Turning right off the main drive, past the Grand Lagoon area, you'll find what is known as "the campground with the most beautiful shade trees." Magnolia Beach Campgrounds, dotted with apartments and cottages throughout the spacious tree-studded grounds, offer tile showers, enclosed toilet and dressing room facilities. Accessible are washers, dryers and utility tables for campers. There are barbecue grills, electric hookups, water and tables at each camp or trailer site.

Also located near Thomas Drive are the Alligator Point Campgrounds, with 175 roomy campsites for trailers, tents, or pick-up campers. All are complete with picnic tables, barbecue grills, electricity and individual running water connections. Strategically located are spotless bath houses with showers or restrooms; electric washers and dryers are also available. The Alligator Point Store has groceries, ice, and all types of fishing tackle. Boats, motors and bait are here along with a children's playground, recreation hall, fishing pier and nature trail. Pets on leash are welcome. Rates are

$2.50 for overnight, $3.00 with electricity; these include water, use of bath houses and all but optional facilities. Reasonable fees are charged for boats, motors, bait, use of washers and dryers.

From the turn-off at Magnolia Beach, Thomas Drive swings around the western edge of the Naval Ship Research and Development Lab, where all types of underwater work and research are constantly underway. Immediately before the intersection of Thomas Drive and US Highway 98 near Hathaway Bridge is the year-old athletic field. Land for the Gulf Coast Midget Football League was donated and developed by area businessmen. Picturesque as any drive on the Gulf Coast, and providing extra interest in housing and recreation for everyone, Thomas Drive is truly becoming another of Panama City's area resort centers.

The beguiling travel writing of "Thomas Drive" may leave the reader breathless with unanswered questions. With whom was Thomas Drive

This 1966 advertisement for the Bunny Club would seem to tempt lawyers from Hugh Hefner's enterprises as well as the castles of Disney. *Courtesy Local History Room, Bay County Public Library.*

competing in the "fun section" competition? And who knew Magnolia Campground as "the campground with the most beautiful shade trees"? Putting aside these puzzling prose poems, the next section, coupled with Kodachrome photographs of families gathered around the tailgate of a 1965 Ford F-150 sporting a diamond-stamped camper top, may incite a mass migration to Camper's Inn, or St. Andrews State Park, the only two tent camping sites left of this group.

Get Away from It All—Conveniently

What more could campers want? Shaded sites, full facilities, good swimming...plus line fishing and a location practically next door to the "World's Most Beautiful Beaches." A tent with a beautiful view tempts campers to stay longer than they had planned...to enjoy the many activities at local campgrounds and near-by recreational centers. Outdoor enthusiasts can enjoy full camping pleasure, boating, fishing and swimming coupled with first rate camp sites when they stay at Magnolia Beach Campgrounds.

Magnolia Beach Cottages and Camp Grounds offered a ready-made camp for postwar vacationers. This ad ran in the late 1960s and early 1970s. *Courtesy Local History Room, Bay County Public Library.*

Fishing off the 450 foot jetty at St. Andrews State Park provides hours of enjoyment for campers in this vacation wonderland.

Florida is a "natural" for campers. Beaches and wooded areas alike provide perfect settings for the ever growing numbers of family groups who prefer to "rough it" on their vacations. Throughout the state you'll find excellent campgrounds, but none better than those in Panama City! Spectacularly-situated areas fill all the needs of these visitors. With facilities ranging from the most primitive surroundings—for a really rugged vacation—to sites with electrical hookups and at-home conveniences.

The innate beauty has been left undisturbed. Huge trees and sparkling waters await families who want to "get away from it all"—conveniently. St. Andrews State Park is one of the most frequently visited campsites in the area. Bordered on the south by the waters of the Gulf of Mexico and on the north by St. Andrews Bay, it boasts a wildlife refuge and some of the area's best fishing at the "jetties" on its 1022 acres of white sandy beaches and wild dunes. It offers a great outdoor atmosphere for a memorable visit. Rates are arranged per day if you wish and electrical hookups are available.

Just around the bend on U.S. 98 off Route 392 and onto Route S392B is Magnolia Beach Campgrounds with two bedroom cottages and efficiency apartments available for those who travel without equipment. Safe swimming for the kids is featured. Some of camping's newest innovations are found at Magnolia Beach. Water hookups are at each campsite, electricity at most: utility and picnic tables are at each site—placed under large shade trees. Barbecue grills, tile showers, enclosed bath houses, private dressing areas and washers and dryers are located in central areas—convenient to all nearby campsites. A camp store offers ice, tackle, bait, boat rentals and a complete line of groceries and camping needs. Small boats can be launched right from the campgrounds; families often spend a day fishing or just boating in the bay. All campgrounds in the Panama City area are located near churches and shopping centers. Facilities are such that the entire family will enjoy a vacation that will be cherished tor many years to come. While dad takes advantage of the fishing, mom can send the kids to a movie or one of the numerous, exciting amusement parks and have her hair done nearby.

Look no further for your campsite dream. For the family that loves outdoor living in unforgettable surroundings, Panama City offers more than any other area on the Gulf Coast. Abandon your everyday cares for a taste of the great outdoors like no other. Spend your vacation camping in Panama City!

What's in a Name?

Sand and shade trees abounded when the navy base was being developed in the late 1940s. The teams there had produced results that had assured its presence here. In the 1950s, they began laying out streets that by the 1960s would be lined with Florida patio homes for the families. Some lived across the street in Woodlawn and some on the lagoon, but everyone traversed the base for shopping and recreation. This witty history of the street names in the new (in 1955) on-base housing first appeared in the laboratory magazine, *The Underseer.*

> *The apparently simple task of choosing street names for the laboratory can run into complications. For example, the monitor* Tecumseh *(commanded by Tunis Craven of "After you, Pilot" fame), looked like a natural. This vessel was sunk by a mine at the Battle of Mobile Bay while assigned to one of the*

Under command of Captain Warfield C. Bennett, the U. S. Navy Mine Defense Laboratory carries on work which encompasses the start-to-finish development of underwater weapons system as they would be needed in total or limited warfare.

scientific seahunters

NAVY MINE DEFENSE LABORATORY

Humming electronic computors and keen analytical minds have joined with the latest military equipment at the Navy Mine Defense Laboratory here in a year-round, continuing study of vital importance to the nation's security. In view of the Soviet Union's estimated 600 submarines and the threat this poses to free world shipping, the development of underwater weapons systems to detect and eliminate mines and torpedoes has paramount importance. This laboratory is the Navy's principal scientific center devoted to this work.

The Laboratory is located on 728 acres one mile west of Panama City on St. Andrew's Bay which provides a well-protected harbor with climactic conditions for year-round sea tests of new weapons.

Started as the Navy Mine Countermeasures station in 1945, the lab was given its present name in 1955. Key work of the lab is done in the Scientific Department staffed by physical scientists and engineers who employ latest electronic and mathematical techniques in studying behavior of under water weapons. Much of their work is highly secret.

The operation includes 105 buildings and $16 million of equipment as well as shore tracking stations, two off-shore "Texas" towers, a group of helicopters, a division of minesweepers and sundry diving facilities. The annual payroll approaches $6 million. • • •

MEETING THE MINE MENACE. Minesweepers, helicopters and off-shore "Texas" towers are all part of the US Navy Mine Defense Laboratory arsenal of equipment.

Small blurb featuring Navy Mine Defense Laboratory. Bay County was justifiably proud of the navy base, permanently established directly southwest of the Hathaway Bridge in 1945. The two large instrumental research platforms in St. Andrews Bay and the Gulf were landmarks for a generation of beachgoers. *Courtesy Local History Room, Bay County Public Library.*

first mine countermeasures missions. However a careful examination of facts shows that the assigned mission had been completed but Craven turned too soon in his eagerness to commence a fire-fight, thus carrying TECUMSEH and himself to destruction in the minefield. So we will not have a Tecumseh Lane.

A number of strongly supported names were obviously chosen to commemorate the discomfiture of those who look down on mine defense as a waste of time and money, especially in peacetime. These were eliminated as were the names of minesweepers whose chief claim to fame was in being sunk by mines.

Many illustrious mine craft were not commemorated because the street name would be associated with the person for whom the vessel had been named rather than the vessel. In one case a most noted DMS bore the name of an officer that U.S. naval historians would like to forget. VERNON stayed on the list because a sample group of laboratory personnel answered without exception that VERNON brought to mind the famous defense laboratory in England. None of them had heard of Admiral "Old Grog" Vernon for whom it was named.

Tom and Anna Watson entertain in their Woodlawn home, 203 Carolyn Avenue, right across the street from work at the navy base, mid-1960s. Louise Percy, Allen Victor, Bob Crispen, Bill Brewer and Bonnie Elkins. *Courtesy Local History Room, Bay County Public Library, Tom Watson.*

When the tentative names were placed on the map of the Laboratory, the task was not complete. A careful check was made to see that Raven Place did not pass though any Scientific area. A similar check was made to be certain that no Supply building bordered Pirate Place. QUAIL, PIGEON and SPARROW could not appear near the new Married Quarters, nor could MAGPIE or CROW. For obvious reasons many of the "pep" names given to distinguished ocean minesweepers were inappropriate. And no, folks, we did not get the name "Solomons Drive" for the main road from Tales of the South Pacific. Ten years ago our Laboratory moved here from its original location at Solomons, Maryland.

UNUSUAL SEA ANIMALS

One young family took great advantage of life in the most beautiful spot in the world. In the 1950s, Roy Martin worked at the fifteen-foot-tall Panama City Beach Pier selling sodas and snacks. Typical beach bum job. However, Roy rigged up a pulley for a dumb waiter so beachgoers wouldn't have to contemplate walking all the way back to the hotel entrance and all the way up the pier to buy a drink from him. This was classic Roy Martin. Lots of folks fished, and locals had guided visiting would-be anglers going back to Jose Massaleno, but none yet with the flash and flair of Roy Martin. He utilized print and television and ran a seafood restaurant and even a fish freak show, all successful in keeping sport fishing, Panama City Beach and Roy Martin in mind. From a late '60s visitors' guide, meet Roy Martin!

Roy Martin added to his collection of 36 world fishing records the 1968 Florida Outdoorsman of the Year award, given by members of the Florida Outdoor Writers Association at their annual meeting in Kissimmee, Florida on June 15. The award is presented each year by the Association to an individual who has contributed to the conservation and wise use of Florida's natural resources.

Though he cannot swim and does not eat fish, Roy Martin is a member of the Fishing Hall of Fame. He has been Mayor of Panama City Beach for the past ten years and has worked actively for conservation legislation; he was able to support this endeavor through knowledge gained from years of working on his own private marine life research projects. His research gained fame when Roy discovered the "Roy Martin Circle" an area which last year yielded the largest blue marlin caught anywhere in Florida. Both director and judge of the Miracle Strip Marlin Tournament held annually

Carol Collins shows off a fine fish caught off the dock in her backyard on the north side of the lagoon, early 1960s. Her parents had built a home and moved the young family from the Alabama Motel, a couple of blocks and several large dunes away. *Courtesy Claudia Shumaker.*

for sports enthusiasts, Roy Martin has many other claims to fame. He is a member of the Bay County Chamber of Sports Committee, a director of the Florida Outdoor Writers Association, and member of the Outdoor Writers Association of America and a fishing expert under contract for 60 national television films on sport fishing.

His first world's record catch was a 49-pound, 15-ounce cobia (ling) which he landed on light casting tackle with an 18 pound test line in April 1952. He landed the fish after a two hour struggle elbow-to-elbow with many fishermen on the Panama City Beach Pier. Checking with the International Game Fish Association as an afterthought, he found that he was on the books. Four weeks later he landed a 197-pound jewfish from the jetties using a 30-pound test line; after two months, a 42-pound, 12-ounce amberjack found itself on the end of his 12 pound test line. Roy's wife, Dolores, holds a record for women in the world-record list—a 5-pound, 1-ounce fish taken on a 50-pound test line—or so her fisherman husband says. However, she does hold two women's world championships for freshwater fishing!

The Martin's own a combination tackle shop and grocery at St. Andrews State park and an apartment complex; they published a Rookie Fishing guide and operate Fishland U.S.A. (Unusual Sea Animals). They are firm believers in conservation, and try to teach all fishermen to throw

The Beach Party (on Thomas Drive), "Open Every Day & Night of the Year," aimed for the younger crowd. In addition to several alliterative activities promised, the ad included "Dancing Alfresco" in what can only be considered suggestive quotation marks. Late 1960s. *Courtesy Local History Room, Bay County Public Library.*

back underdeveloped fish to allow them a chance to grow. Roy estimated last year that he had thrown back about 1½ million pounds of fish in his years as a champion.

One of his largest catches didn't make it into the record book. A 1236-pound manta ray (devil fish) kept him fighting for 14 hours with a medium-heavy rod and 72-pound test line; but rays are not considered game fish. Still, no one doubts that this was one of the largest fish of any kind taken on an artificial lure.

Despite his many awards, Roy Martin maintains that he, like every other fisherman, is still a rookie. "Because our life span is so short, every fisherman is a rookie because he cannot live long enough to enjoy all types and phases of fishing," says the expert. He urges sportsmen to speak to a native fisherman when entering a new area or using a different style of fishing.

The spokesman for the Florida Outdoor Writers Association summed it up at the presentation of the Outdoorsman of the year award to Martin, saying, "Martin, it is true, is a legend—but a living legend."

World Witnesses Growth of Beach

The *Panama City News Herald* is the successor to George and Lillian Wests' *Panama City Pilot*. In the 1980s, the paper ran a column called "Neighbors." This is a profile of Dennis and Martha Rich, longtime beach business owners. Phil Davis spent the afternoon with the Riches at their Panama City Beach souvenir shop.

He Bought the Store

Martha Rich rang up the prices of two large varnished sea shells on her hand crank adding machine at Stuckey's Pecan Shoppe. As she carefully wrapped each shell in white paper, she chatted with the Georgia tourist who was purchasing the mementos.

Meanwhile, her husband, Dennis Rich, gassed up the woman's van, cleaned windows—front and back—and checked the vehicle's oil and water levels.

"That'll be $19.00," Dennis said, stepping from the oppressive summer heat into the store's air conditioning. The tourist paid cash for the shells and handed Martha Rich a credit card for the gas.

Dennis Rich held open the door for the tourist as she left, clutching her bag of Florida treasure.

"Come back and see us," he says cheerfully.

THE SHELL SHOP

Gifts Novelties & Souvenirs

Highway 98—Halfway Between Long Beach and Hathaway Bridge

THE MOST COMPLETE SEA SHELL AND MARINE COLLECTION IN FLORIDA

LIVE SEA HORSES

FREE GIFT

Per Car With Purchase

8014 Highway 98 West Panama City, Florida

Mmm…slightly "off" marine life, too sweet "orange blossoms" and the never-to-be-matched fragrance of Coppertone—nothing can compare to the Shell Shop. How could there *be* this many shells in all the oceans? This ad touts "Live Sea Horses," but what I remember is back scratchers, butt pinchers and, in one shop, a talking minah bird. Early 1970s. *Courtesy Local History Room, Bay County Public Library.*

Dennis and Martha Rich have done this seven days a week for 35 years, except for Christmases. They have worked together for 42 years but they're not bored with it or, as their constant smiles testify, each other.

They enjoy meeting people. And they can't even begin to count how many tourists have stopped in at their store, just west of the intersection of Thomas Drive and U.S. 98.

"I like people," Dennis Rich said. "Ninety nine out of 100 people are nice. I just pass over the few bad apples."

The little Stuckey's has stood like a rock in the stream of development since August 1954. The store is their own, and when money was tight they used to live in a little apartment in the back.

They smile at each other when they talk about the state's aborted plan to have Back Beach Road four-laned before 1959. Surrounding the Stuckey's back then were pine trees and swampland.

Al Boden was one of the men who saw potential in the white sand. He bought a few acres and had two streets laid out. Being a family man who attended First Methodist Church right in the Cove, he named the streets after his blond children, Danny and Nancee. By delightful coincidence, a young matron with a vision, Nancy Bryant Burbage, heard of the offering and put her 10 percent down and paid under fifty dollars a month for a lot to build a "Holiday on the Gulf," so named, in a charming blue and green mosaic. Her son Bob "Butch" Burbage, Max the dachshund, Nancy Bryant Burbage Elliot, daughter Nan Burbage Saddler and Drenda Lawly commemorate being some of the only folks on Thomas Drive, 1970. *Courtesy Nancy Bryant Burbage Elliot.*

The Richs' nearest neighbors were the now closed Indian Post at the Thomas Drive–West U.S. 98 intersection and the Snake-A-Torium, a couple of miles west of U.S. 90. The Snake-A-Torium owner used to trap water moccasins for his business in the swampy area surrounding Stuckey's, the Richs remember.

In those days, it was unusual to see one car pass by the store every 15 minutes, Dennis Rich said. And, "the only things between here and the bridge was some cabins," he said.

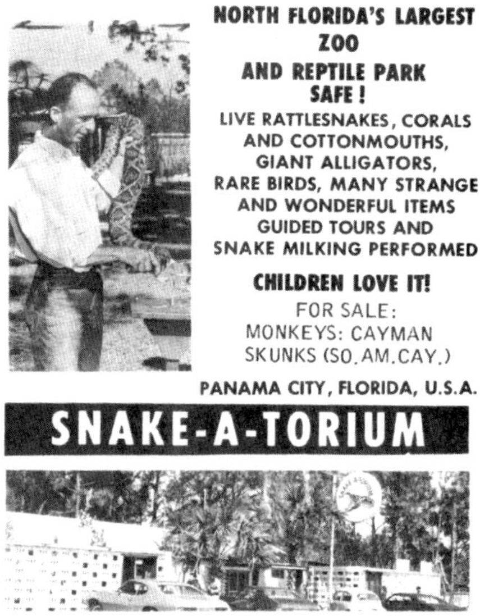

This double ad in a 1972 tourist tabloid showcases the Panama City Beach experience. The Playhouse's distinctive candy-colored signage belied one of the most memorable country bars around. Speaking of signage, the Snake-A-Torium's poised-to-devour cottonmouth lured in countless boys and grown-up boys in the pre–Zoo World days. Next to the photo of a huge rattler being milked, the copy proclaims, "Children Love It!" If there's anything they'd love more, it's probably a monkey or a skunk to take home. *Courtesy Local History Room, Bay County Public Library.*

Today, green space is at a premium from the Stuckey's to the Hathaway Bridge, and hundreds of cars roar by the little blue-and-white shop every minute. The Beachwalk Centre shopping center sits on what used to be the water moccasin swamp.

Back in the 1950s, only cabins were for rent on the beach, Dennis Rich said. It was still a small community and police didn't care if people slept on the beach, a common practice.

"We were the stopping point between Pensacola and Tallahassee," Martha Rich said. "All the college kids used to come by. Now we've seen their children and sometimes their children's children."

The Richs remember the first 40 room motel to appear on the beach—"Everybody thought it was something great," Dennis Rich said.

Now, towering 200 room condos dominate the beach skyline [they had no idea!] *and from the Richs' standpoint, progress is not an improvement.*

"Personally, I'd rather have seen it stay small," he said. "Not as small as it was, but not built up where you can't see. People are just not farsighted enough. I guess that's just human nature."

The Genie! Housed on Signal Hill and originally owned and managed by the Collins family, Don McCoy came to town in 1972 intending to bring LA to lower Alabama. Being an AM daytimer, it went off the air at 4:45 p.m., which may or may not have been they way they did it back in Los Angeles. It was McCoy's first station, and he had fun with it, putting on contests encouraging listeners to answer their telephones, "I listen to WGNE!" bringing in effects on the jocks' voices. One young visitor said he'd feel like he'd really gotten to the beach when he could pick up "the G-g-eeee-n-eeeee" on the car's static-y radio. Jimmy Carter (no, not that one) came down often and visited the eastern end of the beach, sometimes shooting old Super 8 at the State Park, "an oasis in all the hubbub." He loved the reverb crazy "Genie in a lamp" effect and the chart hits of the late 1960s and early 1970s. He is now a well-known broadcaster himself in Nashville, Tennessee. *Author's collection.*

Above: In 1972, Your Complete Vacation Headquarters could be all in this neat little building; even port-a-cribs were available for free. It is now the site of Rick Seltzer Park, as well as one of PCB's first forays into big-time condo building and investing, the Dunes of Panama. *Courtesy Local History Room, Bay County Public Library.*

Opposite below: These trailers on the east end of North Lagoon were just right for visiting teenagers from Dothan. Marie Bryson's uncle Rhett Bryson bought a piece of land in about 1968 and put some trailers there, renting them out to family and others until the late 1970s. Other relatives lived at the end of Dellwood, but the drive down Thomas was just as deserted, with Half Hitch Tackle the only sign of life. The lagoon hadn't been dredged yet and was swampy. Marie and her friends didn't mind at all. *Courtesy Marie Bryson Kelly.*

Dennis and Martha have been married 47 years. "The big 48 is in December," they say, grinning at each other for the umpteenth time during the interview. In those five decades they have raised three children and five grandchildren.

When he's not at Stuckey's, Dennis Rich is involved with the Beach Optimist Club—he has 24 years perfect attendance, was president one year and has been secretary for 22 years.

During World War II, Rich served with the 20th Air Force on Tinian Island, where the Enola Gay was launched on its mission to drop the first atomic bomb on Japan.

"I was on Tinian at the time they flew that atomic bomb," he said. "We didn't know what it was—just a bunch of rumors. We had heard it was a blockbuster-type bomb—bigger than anything."

Regency Towers, ground zero for spring breakers and triathletes alike, is the former site of Addeler's Restaurant and Lounge. It boasted "Live Music Year Round" and "Businessmen's Lunch Every Day." *Courtesy Local History Room, Bay County Public Library.*

After the war, he worked in Stuckey's around Florida and Georgia. At one point he passed up an opportunity to get higher pay as an auto mechanic and he's glad he did it.

Dennis Rich said, "Mr. Stuckey" himself asked if he would like to go into partnership on a Panama City Beach Stuckey's. He took the offer.

"I took what little money I had and opened this store," Dennis Rich said.

"Mr. Stuckey" owned half the business until 1959, when Dennis Rich finally had enough money to follow some advice his father had given him long ago.

"My daddy used to tell me, 'it's better to sell peanuts for yourself, than work for somebody else.'"

He bought the store.

CUB REPORTER GIVEN HER BAPTISM

What a day. On September 24, 1975, Linda Kelley was given on-the-job training with Frank Pericola, the noted sportswriter and editor. Pericola had a scholarship in his name awarded to communications students at Gulf Coast State College;

he loved for young folks to get excited about writing a story, and what a story! It was the day after Hurricane Eloise swept in early Tuesday morning. Winds flattening the shoreline between Panama City Beach and Fort Walton were clocked at 120 to 125 miles an hour. This cub reporter was given her baptism.

> *When I reported to work my first day on Tuesday morning, the day of Hurricane Eloise, the* News Herald *did not have any electrical power, and the phones were working but we could not phone out, which caused a problem in getting the news.*
>
> *Frank Pericola, the editor, and I went around to different places trying to get some reports on the hurricane damages and the situations of the people in the area. We visited Channel 13 TV station. They had just lost their power too and were having difficulties.*
>
> *The Civil Defense Station was running on a generator for its power, and was helping people who had lost their homes or any other serious problems that had arisen from the hurricane. Parts of the Power Company plant were running on generated power, while other parts were left in the dark. They were very busy trying to get power to the hospitals and other places that really needed it. They were trying to get power to everyone and even called in workers from different places.*
>
> *The telephone company was our next place to visit. We arrived there when some of the workers' families were leaving to go back to their own homes. Dick Costello was kind enough to let us borrow his phone to try to get in touch with the* Fort Walton Beach Playground News. *The telephone company was helping the power company as much as possible. Most of the phones could not be fixed until power was restored.*
>
> *From the telephone company we went to the city and county jails. While we were here we listened to a radio announcement on the result of Hurricane Eloise. It did not sound good for the beach at all. We found out that there were not any deaths or anyone hurt. The jail crew informed us that there was quite a lot of looting going on at the beaches.*
>
> *We came back to the* News Herald *to type up what we had learned. The phones were ringing off the hooks with people wanting to know how the situation was around town and on the beaches. We tried to report to them as best we could.*
>
> *The Salvation Army was our last stop. They fed us sandwiches and gave us coffee and milk to drink. They had kept people overnight there, and fed them. Capt. Donald Hall was getting ready to leave to go to Alabama, taking the canteen, filled with food donated by Piggly Wiggly to the people up there that had been hit by Eloise.*

Into every life some rain must fall; this came in the form of Hurricane Eloise on September 23 and 24, 1975. The east end of the beach escaped the brunt of the damage, but poorly constructed buildings and trailers fared poorly. As always, some owners chose not to rebuild, clearing the way for the beginnings of the condo boom. Newby's Beach Supplies, built low, of block, seemed to suffer only damage to its sign. Corner of Thomas Drive and Joan Avenue, September 1975. *Courtesy Florida State Archives.*

> *When we arrived back at the* News Herald *the phone company crew was there fixing up one of the phones so we could call out. Later on in the afternoon the power was restored. And the newspaper was well on its way to getting the next issue together. The reporters started coming in with their stories and pictures of the damage done around town and on the beach. I helped out by answering the telephones so that they would not be bothered as much. Frank and everyone else at the* News Herald *helped me out so I could do what I had to do. The day had been one that I sure wouldn't forget very soon but it was a day full of interesting and new people and things to learn.*

Eloise did quickly what had been repeatedly urged by consumer groups. The 1975 hurricane put a spotlight on safety issues and encouraged people to make hurricane preparedness a priority.

"CAPT. ANDERSON"
DINNER CRUISE BOAT
with
Live Entertainment
Time: 7 to 10 p.m.
Loading Time: 6:15 p.m.
Adult $10.57 Tax .43 Total $11.00
Children $8.65 Tax .35 Total $9.00
Date MAY 31 1975

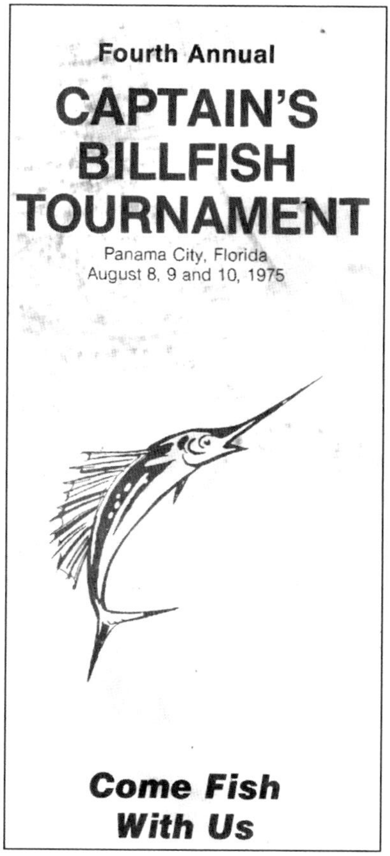

Top: A Captain Anderson excursion, circa 1975. *Courtesy Marie Bryson Kelly.*

Above: A ticket for the much-anticipated "Dinner Boat Cruise." Imagine making it down to the warm breezes of Panama City Beach and getting to board this giant boat, complete with three decks from which to view the turquoise Gulf. And you'd get dinner and entertainment as well! What memories! *Courtesy Marie Bryson Kelly.*

Right: One of the events Bay Point is known for is the Billfish Tournament. Here's a flyer—which actually served as the registration form—for the Fourth Annual, held in 1975. *Courtesy Marie Bryson Kelly.*

Bay Point finally came to fruition in the early 1970s, as depicted in this 1972 ad. The yacht club was laid out in the Mediterranean style now familiar. A plan for the area was drawn up by an Atlanta architectural firm as early as 1958 under the name "Grand Lagoon." *Courtesy Local History Room, Bay County Public Library.*

Worn and weather-beaten, some built cheaply to begin with, old buildings were knocked down and hauled off. Some property owners sold their land, and some built new, large buildings full of rooms designed to be sold individually, to an "investor" and—you'd get the money! Condominium! What could ever go wrong?

WINTER BIRDS ARE A NEW BREED

And there's no danger the snowbird will ever become extinct. By 1982, the northern visitor was being "discovered," even though their antecedents initiated the latter-day tourist tradition on the Gulf beach. Beverly Thompson tells the Panhandle about the coming flock:

There was a time on Panama City Beach when Labor Day meant the sidewalks were pulled in, the CLOSED signs went up and the area slumbered through the winter. For in contrast to Southern Florida the 100 days between Memorial Day and Labor Day were The Season in this Panhandle town. But all this began to change with the advent of the Snowbirds. The term is affectionately applied to the Canadian and Northern visitors who now make the beaches their second home. One of the forerunners of the Snowbirds is Ernie Head from Toronto. He came, he fell in love, and he became a virtual walking Chamber of Commerce. When he returned to Canada after his first visit in 1968, he extolled the beauties of white sugar sand beaches, friendly residents and reasonable prices.

Through the following years, the flock of Snowbirds has swelled to thousands. Ernie and his wife Louise were honored last winter by the Bay County Motel and Restaurant Association for their contribution and dedication. The number of Snowbirds also has increased considerably through the efforts of the Resort Council and the beach branch of the Chamber of Commerce. In recent years the Council has traveled to Northern states, introducing sun-filled Panama City Beach to chilly residents. "You

Aerial view taken by Betty and her husband, pilot Phil Wentzel, in 1978. The St. Louis couple first stayed at the old Beach Colony motel, but walking down the beach they found Holiday on the Beach and fell in love. They built a little house, their "Sand Castle." The neighborhood was close knit and had cookouts and volley ball on the beach. The only other entertainment was Schooner's—just a roof and some rain flaps—and Runaway. *Courtesy Betty Wentzel.*

can't imagine the reaction to our displays," said Larry White, executive director of the Resort Council. "We set up a miniature sand beach with a bikinied sunbather...and a frozen Chicago resident takes one look and decides to head South!" Now Illinois, Ohio, New York and other Northern license plates are a common sight on Panhandle roads during the winter months. A Snowbird Club was started at the Panama City Beach Civic Center in the early 70's. Clubs and organizations sponsor activities including dances and sing-a-longs for the winter visitors.

The flock has been adopted by Rev. Jim Rains; Noah's Ark has become the hub of the Snowbird activities during the winter months. Social gatherings and classes are held nearly every day. A blood pressure clinic is manned by volunteers and at the end of the winter season a huge arts and crafts show is held to display and sell items made during the Snowbirds' stay. Many of the motels have planned an ever-growing number of diversions...shuffleboard teams travel for competitions at the various motels, bridge tournaments are held, and an exciting spring finale is the Fiesta Grand Prix, where senior citizens buzz around the go-cart track vying for the Championship trophy.

The winter season is being discovered by residents of nearby states as well as Northerners. Many have found the balmy days of late fall and early winter much to their liking. The maddening crowds of summer have disappeared, traffic flows smoothly, the soft white sands and the sparkling blue-green waters of the Gulf hold a special charm. "I love to come this time of year," said one visitor. "It's serene and peaceful...as near paradise as you will ever find."

Each year more activities are being planned to extend The Season on the Panhandle beaches. The fifth annual Sunfest was held in September. The juried arts and crafts show attracts artists from all over Florida and from many neighboring states. Thousands of visitors flock to Panama City Beach in October for the Indian Summer Seafood Festival, a two day celebration of food, fun, musical entertainment, parades, arts and crafts shows and displays by Armed Forces units. Early in 1982 the first Sea and Sky Celebration was held, and officials plan to make it an annual spring affair. The 100-day season has been gradually extended as more and more people discover the Panhandle area which once was Florida's best kept secret.

By the twenty-first century, the Gulf beach was a secret no more. Major mass media exposure coupled with sustained growth in the southern real estate market had put the little time-warped tourist mecca on the slightly rearranged map. In 1970, the new city of Panama City Beach was incorporated, consisting of several of the smaller towns established from the 1953 incorporation brouhaha. The Beach, the Beaches, Panama City Beach—what have you—the area was ready to take its seat at the grown-ups table. In 2001, the Bay County Chamber of Commerce sponsored *The Rich Heritage of Panama City Beach and Communities of Bay County*, with business profiles penned by Paul Cox and stories written by two Bay County historians, native son and legislator Jack Mashburn and local author Marlene Womack. This profile of George Butchikas and his twenty-thousand-pound baby, Angelo's, originally appeared in this volume:

> *"Broiling over an open fire stands, in my opinion, as the remote starting point and the very genesis of our art. It has the primeval notion of our forefathers' drive for progress; and motivated by an instinctive desire to eat with greater pleasure. It was the first culinary method ever employed and, in my opinion, has never been improved upon."*
>
> *Those were the enlightening words of Angelo Gus Butchikas, longtime Bay County restaurateur and the founder of Angelo's Steak Pit who died at a much-too-early age of 43 in a car accident in 1963. Today, George Butchikas carries on the tradition of fine foods his dad built after opening Angelo's Steak Pit in what was formerly the 98 Club in May of 1958. "You won't get a bum steer here and that's no bull" might sound like a cliché, but it typifies the high esteem Angelo's enjoys in Bay County and with tourists from all over the country. Located two miles west of the Hathaway Bridge in Panama City Beach, Angelo's boasts clientele of literally millions, serving only the finest choice steaks, chicken, ribs and seafood cooked to renowned perfection over the restaurant's famous open hickory pits while you watch. "We serve more than 200,000 people each season," George Butchikas said. That, despite the fact that Angelo's is open only from the middle of March until the first week of October. The restaurant located on one of the main arteries leading to the beach, employs 150 people and it takes every one of them. We have tried staying open longer but with school starting earlier each year it has taken away from the family vacation and has not been busy enough to stay open.*
>
> *To say that Angelo's steaks are different would be an understatement. "We cook our steaks on hickory and oak wood and one of our specialties is a 32-ounce T-Bone," George revealed. Little wonder that most people who come to the popular restaurant order steaks. While Angelo's is one of the finest restaurants in the Florida Panhandle, it also is one of the most*

unique. Named for Angelo Gus Butchikas, Big Gus, a 20,000-pound steer in front of the building, has become quite popular over the years and has been chosen the leading landmark in Bay County. "We got Big Gus as an eyecatcher in 1970," George said. "They were four-laning Highway 98 and we felt people would be whizzing by so fast, they might miss us. They certainly have an identifying mark in Big Gus." George acquired Gus in an unusual way. "We had to redesign that bull to make it a steer, but Big Gus has been part of our success ever since," Angelo's owner pointed out.

When you enter the lobby at Angelo's, you are greeted by the Prospector, a lonely ragamuffin in a chair who actually talks to you. "I was going to a lot of restaurant shows and I was at this show in Orlando in 1997 when I saw this man," George said. "I thought it would be good for advertising and people really like it. We even have a drink named for the Prospector and his picture is on our menu." George has been the sole owner of Angelo's since 1989 when he bought brother Chris's share of the business. George said he figured it out and that the average employee has been at the restaurant for 15 years. Wilma Fuller, pretty much a landmark herself, has been there since 1962.

George, carrying on the business philosophy of his father, seldom misses a day being in the office at Angelo's. "Sometimes I take off a night or two, but I am always here during the daytime," he said. Good food and fine restaurants have traditionally been a part of the family.

This now nostalgic entry appears as well:

The Treasure Ship, on Grand Lagoon in Panama City Beach, is a majestic 200-foot long replica of a 17th century Spanish galleon similar to that of English adventurer, Sir Francis Drake's ship, The Golden Hind. Ships like this served both the Spanish, who looted the New World in the 17th and 18th centuries and the pirates who in turn looted the Spanish. They were known as treasure ships for they brought back cargo worth millions to their respective sovereigns.

The Treasure Ship was designed to give free reign to your imagination. Walk her decks, explore her hold, sample her wares, eat, drink and be merry! For here, everyone's childhood fantasy of pirates and adventures on the high seas is made real. Swash a little, buckle if you must, be a pirate, the fair maiden, a cabin boy or a king. Finger your silver, toast Her Royal Majesty, celebrate your latest victory, forget defeat. Climb her decks, sight her cannons, lash yourself to the mast in the driving wind. Enjoy the Treasure Ship, it was built for you!

The Dock Level of the Treasure Ship was operated as a popular nightspot called The Brig for many years, but has recently been transformed with Caribbean flair into Hook's Grille & Grog. Hook's features inside and outside dockside dining and is open for lunch and dinner. The well thought-out menu features outstanding offerings of local seafood and Certified Angus Beef dishes. A wide variety of appetizers, entrees and desserts keep a steady clientele of locals and visitors alike. Tropical drinks from the bar are made with fresh-squeezed citrus.

On Level II, in the main body of the ship, you'll find the Main Dining Room. Every seat offers an outstanding waterfront view of all the activity on Grand Lagoon. It's a favorite spot for families as the kids enjoy the pirates that freely roam throughout the restaurant, telling their tall tales, painting little faces and creating balloon art. The family atmosphere is colorful and creative, but does not overshadow the culinary talents of Chef Dee Brown when it comes to good food. Dee's award-winning cuisine has earned national attention. The success starts with the ultimate selection of fresh local seafood and masterful preparation methods that make The Treasure Ship a must for thousands of visitors each year.

On Level III, the Deck Bar has been recently renovated to provide a spacious multilevel entertainment venue. This is the highest lookout point on Grand Lagoon. Live music is featured nightly during the high season. The family will enjoy the blasts of cannon fire as the pirates volley with the ships on the lagoon. The Pirate's Playroom Arcade is a popular spot to test your skills on today's newest video games. The Treasure Ship Gift Shop is open year round with a great selection of souvenirs that will remind you of your wonderful visit to Panama City Beach.

In addition to The Treasure Ship's restaurants and entertainment offerings, the dock below hosts charter fishing boats, sightseeing boats and day-trips to provide you with lots of fun on the water.

In 2010, the Treasure Ship succumbed to the depredations of age—not barnacles or wood worms, but rather, 1970s' wiring lost the battle with the digital age. No fast-paced business like the Treasure Ship could run without a dozen computers and electronic cash registers. On April 28, employees had readied their posts for another busy spring evening when the darkened ship began to fill with smoke. By that evening the county and, thanks to the magic of Facebook, the whole Southeast was in mourning. Many folks had come to the Treasure Ship for their first date, a prom, had a first job here and come on—it was a big brown ship on the side of the road! Moms have to visit Captain Anderson's, kids have to go to the "pirate ship" and have their picture taken in the stocks. In a few years, the kids will graduate to La Vela, where they can have humiliating photos taken on the dance floor and posted on the Internet for all to see.

So this is the east end ten years into the twenty-first century. One hundred years ago, carefree northerners rode the "Gallberry Special" down from Dothan to Panama City's little wooden depot on the bay. How could they even notice the dock when they smelled salt in the air, felt the warm soft breeze on their cheeks and saw that expanse of blue and white in front of their eyes? They were delighted to hire a boat to take them out to see those white sands and eager to pay for a book of photographs of the trip.

The wonder never ceases. A hardened college girl squeals with delight at the incredibly clear water—a raccoon, a dolphin. Young men who have come out on the beach to "GET WASTED" get sidetracked instead talking to an older man, who couldn't help remarking on the group's beach towel—that's *his* alma mater, too.

The 1980s brought unprecedented non-wartime growth to the Southeast, and Panama City Beach grew proportionately. Ralph Bingham had been visiting the area with his dad, Ralph Bingham, since the 1940s, and he and his wife, Dorothy, picked the cutest lot on the east end and started building. The whole family worked together and turned a little Jim Walter home into a comfortable cottage. They plowed back the titi and the trees filled in the rest, creating a cozy hideaway on the lagoon. *Courtesy Ralph and Dorothy Bingham.*

This 1980s flyer shows LaVela's transition from LaVela Beach Club to the "Party People" we know today. *Courtesy Local History Room, Bay County Public Library.*

The cobalt bay, the jade green gulf ever remain, but wind, water and time erode old landmarks and entire islands, all the while creating new islands and landmarks. Men come in and devise easier paths and cut and dredge and dynamite straightaway. The patient waves rhythmically wash the sands back to their appointed shoreline. Castles are built of the sand, tall, intricate, a marvel to behold. The next day's tide, an afternoon squall—the castles are no more.

As this editor left a contributor's home one afternoon, the thought occurred: "Writing a book is the price I pay to meet these people." So many

Pineapple Willie's is now the home of the one-hundred-foot pier, in the location of the Panama City Beach Hotel. This ad dates from the 1980s, in its twenty-five to forty-five age group days. Now there's hardly a teenager in the Southeast who doesn't either have or want a Pineapple Willie's T-shirt. *Courtesy Local History Room, Bay County Public Library.*

shared a story or a photo, passed along a phone number; everyone had a compelling story, something to make the author laugh aloud.

James Sowell recalled an incident from the early '50s:

> *We were out* [fishing in St. Andrews Bay] *getting mullet and salting it down, you know, and my dad says, "Here," handing me a small armload of fish. "Take these over to Teddy."* [see "If There Were No Fools, There'd Be No Fun"] *Well, I was about ten years old and you know how some kids are, I was kind of scared of the old man, he had that long beard, but I got in my boat and rowed over there to where he had that little lean-to and his boat, and he was sitting out there. I glanced over at Teddy to tell him here was his fish so I could leave, and when I looked, he had one of those old wild hogs from over there, and it was laid out flat beside him. Teddy had a long stick and was scratching that old hog's stomach with the stick.*

One hundred years before that story took place, a noted female writer sometimes called the Harriet Beecher Stowe of the South, Caroline Hentz, stayed on the bay at the old Governor Clark house. She looked out on the horizon right over the sand pines that would shelter Teddy Tollofson. She

WJHG-TV built a new studio on Front Beach Road in 1997 and posted this TV-riffic advertisement in a visitors' guide. *Courtesy Local History Room, Bay County Public Library.*

wrote and was quoted to good effect by the old editor himself, George West: "Come to the piazza that faces the beach, and you can look out on an ocean of molten gold, crimsoned here and there by the rays of the setting sun, and here and there melting off into a kind of burning silver."

Do come stay and see our fiery golden sunsets.

She continues, "We too are passing on…and the waves of time that are rolling behind us will wash away the print of our footsteps, and others will follow…but few will be tossed on stormier seas, or be anchored at last in a more blissful haven."

In spite of the ugly shadow cast by the BP Deepwater Horizon oil explosion of 2010 and an eroding economy, (both, incidentally, situations weathered by the peninsula several times before), this corner of the county is still a blissful haven.

Come back and see us.

Selected Bibliography

Adams, William Taylor. *Stand by the Union.* Boston: Horace Partridge, 1891.

Conn Survey City Directory. Panama City, FL: Mullin-Kille Co. & Panama City News Herald, 1948.

Cox, Paul, Jack Mashburn and Marlene Womack. *The Rich Heritage of Panama City Beach and Communities of Bay County*. Montgomery, FL: Community Heritage Publications, 2001.

Davis, William Watson. *The Civil War and Reconstruction in Florida.* New York: Columbia University, 1913.

Holley, Richard. *The Last Voyage of the S.S. Tarpon*. Lynn Haven, FL: Fishermen's Footprints, LLC, 2007.

Houpt, Ann Pratt. St. Andrews Waterfront Project. *St. Andrews.* Charleston, SC: Arcadia Publishing, 2007.

Hutchison, Ira. *Some Who Passed This Way.* Panama City, FL, 1972.

Knight, Lucien Lamar. *A Standard History of Georgia and Georgians.* Chicago: Lewis Publishing Company, 1917.

Moore, Clarence, David Brose and Nancy White. Introduction to *The Northwest Florida Expeditions of Clarence Bloomfield Moore.* Birmingham: University of Alabama Press, n.d.

Morris, Allen. *The Florida Handbook.* N.p.: Peninsular Publishing Company, 1993.

Murphree, Ridgeway Boyd. *Rebel Sovereigns: The Civil War Leadership of Governors John Milton of Florida and Joseph E. Brown of Georgia, 1861–1865.* N.p., 2006.

Panama City Pilot. flhiddentreasures.com.

Powell, Arthur Gray. *I Can Go Home Again.* Chapel Hill, NC, 1943. Reprinted, 1984.

Shepherd, D. William. *The Early Years of the "Navy Lab": A History.* Tallahassee, FL: self-published, 2005.

Warwick, Ann Williams. *Tides.* Panama City, FL: Boyd Brothers, 1982.

Waters, Glenda A. *Panama City.* Charleston, SC: Arcadia Publishing, 2008.

West, George Mortimer. *St. Andrews, Florida.* St. Andrews, FL: Panama City Publishing Company, 1922.

Williams, John Lee. *Territory of Florida.* N.p.: A.T. Goodrich, 1837.

Womack, Marlene. *The Bay Country of Northwest Florida.* Apalachicola: New Hope Press, 1998.

———. *War Comes to Florida's Northern Gulf Coast.* Panama City, FL: self-published, 2002.

About the Author

Jeannie Weller Cooper was born in Atlanta, Georgia. She was educated in Fayetteville and Statesboro. She moved with her family to Panama City, Florida, in 1999 and has enjoyed participating in environmental and educational groups, including the Historical Society of Bay County. Cooper produces multimedia educational programs for schools and civic groups and has written weekly columns for online journals, print magazines, radio and newspaper. *Panama City's Historic Neighborhoods: The Cove* (Arcadia Publishing) was published in 2002. She has two daughters, one cat and a snail and lives on the blissful haven of Grand Lagoon.